ROUTLEDGE LIBRARY EDITIONS: INDUSTRIAL ECONOMICS

Volume 26

PRODUCTIVITY ANALYSIS

PRODUCTIVITY ANALYSIS
An Empirical Investigation

DORIS YI-HSIN WANG

Routledge
Taylor & Francis Group

LONDON AND NEW YORK

First published in 1996 by Garland Publishing, Inc.

This edition first published in 2018
by Routledge
2 Park Square, Milton Park, Abingdon, Oxon OX14 4RN

and by Routledge
711 Third Avenue, New York, NY 10017

Routledge is an imprint of the Taylor & Francis Group, an informa business

British Library Cataloguing in Publication Data
A catalogue record for this book is available from the British Library

ISBN: 978-1-138-30830-5 (Set)
ISBN: 978-1-351-21102-4 (Set) (ebk)
ISBN: 978-1-138-56930-0 (Volume 26) (hbk)
ISBN: 978-0-203-70431-8 (Volume 26) (ebk)

Publisher's Note
The publisher has gone to great lengths to ensure the quality of this reprint but points out that some imperfections in the original copies may be apparent.

Disclaimer
The publisher has made every effort to trace copyright holders and would welcome correspondence from those they have been unable to trace.

PRODUCTIVITY ANALYSIS

AN EMPIRICAL INVESTIGATION

DORIS YI-HSIN WANG

GARLAND PUBLISHING, Inc.
NEW YORK & LONDON / 1996

Library of Congress Cataloging-in-Publication Data

Wang, Doris Yi-Hsin, 1958–.
    Productivity analysis : an empirical investigation / Doris Yi-
Hsin Wang.
       p.   cm. — (Garland studies on industrial productivity)
    Includes bibliographical references and index.
    ISBN 0-8153-2015-9 (alk. paper)
    1. Industrial productivity—Mathematical models.
2. Industrial productivity—United States—Case studies. 3. United
States—Manufactures—Capital productivity—Case studies.
4. Research, Industrial—Economic aspects—United States—Case
studies. I. Title. II. Series.
HB241.W348 1996
338'.06—dc20   95-47463

Printed on acid-free, 250-year-life paper
Manufactured in the United States of America

Contents

List of Tables

List of Figures

Acknowledgments

First of all, I would like to express my sincere gratitude to Dr. Donald L. Madden and Dr. Stuart B. Keller. They provided unreserved assistance and insightful guidance from the very first day, and had kindly consented to undertake the supervision of my work until its completion. Their constructive suggestions and constant encouragement had significantly facilitated the successful completion of this dissertation.

In addition, I wish to express my deep love and appreciation to my husband Alex, my sons, Anthony, Andrew and Alan, and my parents, Chun-E Wang and Mei-Yuan Wang for their love and support throughout these years.

Productivity Analysis

I

Introduction to the Study

Over the last several years, productivity improvement has become an increasingly vital economic issue for both the United States and individual firms. Many prominent economists in the area of productivity research have discussed the growing evidence of declining productivity in the United States and the reasons behind it. They have pointed out that productivity growth slowed in the late 1960s and then actually declined at the end of 1970s, especially after the oil embargo and the associated acceleration in inflation. Emphasizing these declines even further, Gale [1980:78] commented that "the need for productivity improvement may be the most pressing domestic [U.S.] economic problem."

AN OVERVIEW OF RECENT PRODUCTIVITY TRENDS

The economics literature reveals clearly that productivity improvement in the United States has declined dramatically since 1973 (Kendrick, 1980). The investment climate of the 1970s was much less favorable than in preceding periods because accelerating inflation was being exacerbated by the oil embargo (Kendrick, 1984). Table 1 shows total factor productivity indexes for both the overall business economy and the manufacturing sector from 1948 to 1987. While productivity performance increased consistently in the U.S. business economy from 1948 to 1968, a few declines did occur in the manufacturing sector during this time frame. After 1968, however, the business economy also experienced occasional declines.

The range of total factor productivity indexes for the business economy and the manufacturing sector reveals improvements in every decade. However, total factor productivity in the manufacturing sector improved more dramatically than that of the business economy in the last two decades. In the 1980s the productivity of the manufacturing sector began to outpace that of the business economy. As shown in

Table 1, the range of productivity measures in the manufacturing sector was almost three times that of the business economy during the 1980-1987 period.

Table 1
Total Factor Productivity in the U.S.
(1977=100)

Year	Business Economy	Range in Each Decade	Manufacturing Sector	Range in Each Decade
1948	55.1		55.0	
1949	55.2		56.4	
1950	59.5*		59.8*	
1951	61.9		62.2	
1952	63.6		63.1	
1953	65.7		64.5	
1954	65.9		64.3	
1955	68.1		67.5	
1956	68.8		66.7	
1957	70.0		67.5	
1958	71.0		65.8	
1959	73.6**	14.1	69.4**	9.6
1960	74.4*		69.4*	
1961	76.3		70.7	
1962	78.8		73.8	
1963	81.5		78.6	
1964	84.7		82.1	
1965	87.1		84.3	
1966	89.2		85.1	

Notes: Indexes of total factor productivity are measured in percentage and are published from the American Productivity Center. One asterisk (*) indicates the minimum index in each decade. Two asterisks (**) indicate the maximum index in each decade.

Table 1 (Continues)
Total Factor Productivity in the U.S.
(1977=100)

Year	Business Economy	Range in Each Decade	Manufacturing Sector	Range in Each Decade
1967	90.7		84.0	
1968	92.7**		86.1	
1969	92.4	18.3	86.6**	17.2
1970	91.8*		85.0*	
1971	93.7		88.5	
1972	96.4		92.6	
1973	98.3		97.5	
1974	95.2		93.0	
1975	95.2		92.3	
1976	98.0		96.9	
1977	100.0		100.0	
1978	101.3**		101.6**	
1979	99.8	9.5	101.0	16.6
1980	98.1*		98.8*	
1981	98.6		100.0	
1982	96.5		99.2	
1983	99.0		104.9	
1984	102.2		111.8	
1985	104.0		116.2	
1986	105.9		119.3	
1987	106.8**	8.7	123.1**	24.3

Notes: Indexes of total factor productivity are measured in percentage and are published from the American Productivity Center. One asterisk (*) indicates the minimum index in each decade. Two asterisks (**) indicate the maximum index in each decade.

This study focuses on possible reasons for these improvements in U.S. manufacturing industries. Specifically examined are relationships between increased investments in research and development projects and capital improvements and changes in productivity and profitability, and relationships between productivity changes and profitability changes in selected manufacturing industries and companies. Together, these exploratory investigations can perhaps lead to improved planning and control models throughout this important segment of the U.S. economy.

RATIONALE FOR THE STUDY

Kendrick [1984] suggests that the chief cause of productivity improvement in the overall business economy over the long run is the cost-reducing innovation in technology. During the 1970s, American businesses faced not only inflation and high interest rates, but also began to face increasing international competition. The increasing level of competitiveness since that time has forced managers to cut costs, raise productivity, and show more concern for customer needs. To survive in the international market (i.e., to compete more effectively against low-cost, high-quality foreign competitors), manufacturing companies have been forced to improve their production processes by increasing research and development investments and capital expenditures (Howell et al., 1987). Due to the increasing importance of these catalyst financial commitments, managers of manufacturing companies have become much more interested in the impacts of such investments on changes in productivity and profitability.

STATEMENT OF THE PROBLEM

Since many manufacturing companies commit to substantial investments, the return on these catalyst financial commitments becomes critical for business survival and/or success. From a management accounting perspective, a company is assumed to increase its investments in research and development projects and better equipment in order to improve productivity and thereby achieve desired levels of profitability. Theoretically, increased investments in research projects and equipment are thus expected to improve productivity and profitability by achieving the necessary cost-reducing innovation in technology (Kendrick,1984).

To evaluate investment performance, management accountants need information about the effects of substantial investments on changes in productivity and profitability. Also important are assessments of the impacts of productivity improvements on profitability. The availability of improved information on these relationships may allow U.S. manufacturing companies to learn more about investment performance of their companies and competitors. Ultimately, these U.S. manufacturing companies should be able to compete more effectively in the international marketplace.

The problem is that management accountants frequently do not have access to enough data for comparing their company's performance to others in the same industry. This exploratory study is intended to build a bridge between these needs and currently available databases through the use of publicly available data. If successful, this study should enable management accountants to move forward in developing more sophisticated planning and control models for the above purposes.

OBJECTIVES OF THE STUDY

The primary objective of this exploratory study is to examine empirically relationships between changes in catalyst financial commitments (i.e., research and development projects and capital improvements) and productivity/profitability changes, and relationships between productivity changes and profitability changes in selected manufacturing industries and companies. Specific attention is focused on identifying, clarifying, and investigating empirically the effects of increases in substantial investments on changes in productivity and profitability. Theoretically, both the development of good quality products and the installation of better equipment would be expected to improve company productivity and profitability. In seeking to determine the impacts of substantial investments, this study attempts to answer the following questions: 1) What are the impacts of changes in catalyst financial commitments on productivity changes? 2) Are there significant relationships between productivity changes and profitability changes? 3) What are the impacts of changes in catalyst financial commitments on profitability changes? 4) Do time lags exist between changes in catalyst financial commitments and productivity/profitability changes for the first and second year after the year of investment?

THE STUDY FOCUS MODEL

This study is focused on the need to improve productivity and profitability in the United States. The literature suggests that increases in substantial investments (i.e., research and development projects and capital equipment) may lead to improvements in productivity. Other relevant studies indicate that improved productivity may contribute to profitability increases. Further, increases in substantial investments may also have direct impacts on profitability. The Gold model is used as the theoretical foundation for the Study Focus Model (Figure 1), that illustrates five key relationships among four variables.

Figure 1
The Study Focus Model

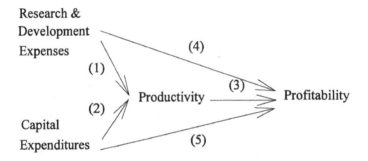

The 1980-1989 time frame was selected for this study for three reasons: (1) data availability, (2) manufacturing productivity improvements, and (3) the 1974 accounting standard change which may have impacted on management's investment decisions throughout the late 1970s. The most current data in the COMPUSTAT II file are for 1989. As is shown in Table 1, total factor productivity for the manufacturing sector outpaced that of the overall business economy in this period. This time frame comes after the promulgation of Statement of Financial Accounting Standards No. 2, Accounting for Research and Development Costs which required that virtually all research and development expenditures be expensed in the period of the outlay (hence the use of the term, "Research and Development Expense" in this study). It was effective for fiscal years beginning on or after January 1, 1975, and may have impacted temporarily on some research and development investment decisions by management. Thus, the investigation of the 1980-1989 period should mitigate the impacts of this confounding variable.

DEFINITIONS AND MEASURES OF VARIABLES

The following working definitions are utilized throughout this study. The definitions of Research and Development Expenses and Capital Expenditures are from the manual of COMPUSTAT. The definitions of Productivity and Profitability are taken from other research studies; their sources are indicated. For each variable in the study, the base year is 1980. Measurement of each variable is detailed below.

Research and Development Expenses include all research costs incurred during the year that relate to the development of new products or services. Changes in Research and Development Expenses (C_RD) are used in this study and are measured as follows:

C_RD(%)=(Current R&D - Base Year R&D) / Base Year R&D.

Capital Expenditures are items that are reflected in the dollar amount spent on the construction and/or acquisition of property, plant, and equipment in a given year. Changes in Capital Expenditures (C_CAP) are applied in this study and measured as follows:

C_CAP(%)=(Current Cap Exp - Base Cap Exp) / Base Cap Exp.

Productivity is usually defined in the economics literature as a ratio of output to input. Two types of productivity measures are discussed in this study: partial productivity ratios and total factor productivity ratios. This study follows Kendrick's [1984] productivity definition, that is, the ratio of output to inputs of labor and other resources. Total factor productivity value in dollars as calculated by the American Productivity Center model is used in this study; the model is discussed in the next section of this chapter.

Profitability indicates how well the enterprise has operated during the year. Traditional profitability analyses consist of many ratios, such as Return on Assets (i.e., the Dupont model), return on sales, and gross profit. Gold [1955] developed a basic model that attributes changes in the ratio of profit to total investment to five areas of performance: product price, unit costs, facilities utilization, productivity of facilities and equipment, and the allocation of investment resources between capital goods working capital. In the Gold model, changes in the rate of profit on total investment are influenced by the interactions of changes in these five factors. In this study, Return on Assets (Net Operating Income / Total Assets) is used as the profitability measurement because of the dominant position of this measure in management accounting literature. Changes in Return on Assets (C_ROA) are used as profitability measures and computed as follows:

C_ROA(%)=(Current ROA - Base Year ROA) / Base Year ROA.

PRODUCTIVITY MEASUREMENT

Kendrick [1961:32] states, "The story of productivity, the ratio of output to input, is at heart the record of man's effort to raise himself from poverty." Output is the amount of goods and services produced, and input includes the quantity of labor, capital, and other resources used to produce the output (Baumol and McLennan, 1985). When given amounts of input produce larger quantities of output (or when output can be maintained with reduced levels of input), productivity has increased.

At the national level, output is a measure of the total output of the economy, such as gross national product (GNP) or net national product (NNP); components of the input are materials, labor, and capital (Fusfeld, 1972). At industry and firm levels of activity, Kendrick [1984] defines sales revenue as the output and all costs incurred to produce that output as input. Kendrick's definitions of output and input are also applied in the American Productivity Center (APC) measurement system that serves as a frame of reference in this study. The APC model, focuses on the gross profit measure, a critical measure emphasized throughout the management accounting literature.

With regard to productivity measures Craig and Harris [1973] identify two distinct types of ratios, total productivity (or "total factor productivity") and partial productivity. The ratio of total output to the sum of all inputs is total factor productivity. A partial productivity measure is derived by dividing total output by a single input. Baumol and McLennan [1985] note that total factor productivity is the better measure of an economy's efficiency because it measures the ratio of output to the sum of all basic inputs. Kendrick [1984:47] recommends total factor productivity as a measure of the efficiency of a business as a whole, and points out that "some part of the increase in output per labor hour has reflected the substitution of capital for labor, and the real unit cost reduction is a mirror image of total factor productivity." Many management accounting studies also suggest using total factor productivity as a measure of productivity (Wait 1980; Mammone,1980a; Brayton, 1985).

Productivity measurement is used to evaluate changes of output-input ratios in the production process. Kendrick [1980:11] emphasizes that "the ratio of output to input at a point in time has no meaning." Wait [1980:25] also states that "productivity has essentially no meaning except on a comparative basis." Consequently, productivity ratios are meaningful only in measuring changes over a period or for identifying differences among plants or firms producing identical goods in the same industry.

Most researchers recommend total factor productivity as a measure for the efficiency evaluation of an entire business entity (Kendrick, 1984; Wait, 1980). Nevertheless, productivity measurement does not replace traditional financial measures; instead, this tool can be a useful supplement enabling the analyst to separate variances due to relative price changes from those due to changes in production efficiency (Davis, 1955; Kaplan, 1973). With regard to evaluating productivity accurately, Wait [1980:26] points out that "the development of an appropriate overall measure of productivity change is a current challenge for the management accountant."

THE APC MODEL

A frequently used model for measuring productivity changes was created by the American Productivity Center (APC) in the early 1980s. The APC model is gross-profit oriented, focuses on total factor productivity, and uses a single-step deflation method. The APC model is shown as follows:

$$\text{Productivity} = C_B[(S_t^B / S_B) - (C_t^D / C_B)]$$

where

C_B : Costs in the base period,

C_t^B : Costs in the period t deflated to the base period,

S_B : Sales in the base period,

S_t^D : Sales in period t deflated to the base period.

For an empirical study, data availability is a major concern in model selection. The APC model uses only sales, cost of good sold, and deflating factor. These data that can be obtained from publicly available sources. The APC model is used by many manufacturing companies because of the simplicity of its single-step deflation method. In this study, the APC model is used to measure total factor productivity.

METHODOLOGY CONSIDERATIONS

This study examines the relationships between changes in catalyst financial commitments and changes in productivity and profitability, and relationships between productivity changes and profitability changes. The scope is limited to industries, and companies within these selected industries, that satisfy all the criteria specified for analysis purposes. Relevant criteria are described in the following section. Using these selected industries and companies as the frame of reference, all analyses relate to the investigation of five relationships among four variables, as shown in the Study Focus Model (Figure 1).

Sample Selection Procedures

The population for this study comprises all companies in COMPUSTAT II, a database containing twenty years of financial data (1970-1989) for 2,478 companies in 382 industries. The time frame of this study is limited to the ten-year period 1980-1980 for reasons previously given. The sample satisfies both industry selection criteria and company selection criteria for this study.

Industry selection criteria are (1) type of industry, (2) annual amount of Research and Development Expenses, (3) annual amount of Capital Expenditures, and (4) capacity utilization rate. According to the U.S. Department of Commerce system, an industry with the first two digits of its Standard Industry Classification (SIC) code in the range 20-39 is a manufacturing industry. Only manufacturing industries, both nondurable and durable goods industries as classified by the Bureau of the Census, are included in this study. The nondurable industries are the industries for which the first two digits of the SIC codes are 20-23 and 26-31. The durable industries are those for which the first two digits of the SIC codes are 24,25, and 32-39.

The findings of the Howell and Soucy [NAA 1987] study indicate that manufacturers are expending a "significant" portion of available cash on advanced manufacturing technology if they are spending $1-$10 million annually on such technology. Thus, only manufacturing industries that invest a large amount in research and development activities and capital expenditures are included in the sample. In the entire population, approximately 20% of the 382 industries have average annual research and development expenses in excess of $10 million, and approximately 60% of the 382 industries have average annual capital expenditures in excess of $10 million. Consequently, for each selected industry both the mean of annual research and development expenses and the mean of annual capital expenditures over the ten-year period 1980-1989 must be greater than $10 million.

In addition, the capacity utilization rate of each selected industry is greater than the average capacity utilization rate for its subgroup (nondurable or durable goods industries). Capacity utilization is the ratio of actual to capacity output. Bauer and Deily [1988] note that the capacity utilization rate published by the U.S. Census Bureau is one of the most widely disseminated indexes of capacity utilization. The Census Bureau prepares the *Survey of Plant Capacity*, which covers about 450 manufacturing industries at the four-digit Standard Industrial Classification code level.

Two separate capacity utilization measures are calculated in the *Survey*, the preferred rate and the practical rate. The preferred rate is the market value of actual output divided by the value of preferred output. The practical rate is the value of actual output divided by the value of practical output. Practical output is defined as the greatest output that the plant could achieve within the framework of a realistic work pattern. Preferred output is an expected level of output that is less than practical output. Therefore, the practical rate is lower than the preferred rate in the *Survey*. In this study, the practical rate of capacity utilization as published in the *Survey* is used for industry selection because over time the practical rate is the more stable of these two measures.

After specific manufacturing industries have been selected, individual companies are included in the sample after satisfying four company selection criteria: (1) annual amount of Research and Development Expenses, (2) annual amount of Capital Expenditures, (3) availability of complete 10-year data, and (4) no change in inventory valuation methods. In the population for the period 1980-1989, approximately 20% of the 2478 companies have average research and development expenses greater than $1 million per year, and approximately 70% have average capital expenditures greater than $1 million per year. For the selected companies, both the mean of annual research and development expenses and the mean of annual capital expenditures over the ten-year period, 1980-1989, must be greater than $1 million. After these criteria are satisfied, only companies with complete 10-year data and those that had no change in inventory valuation methods over the 1980-1989 period are included in the sample. As a result, the research sample comprises 77 companies in 20 industries from the population after all selection criteria are satisfied.

Analytical Procedures

To accomplish the objectives of this study, five hypotheses are to be tested in each subgroup (e.g., industry and company) of this study as follows:

H_{01}: Changes in Research and Development Expenses are not related to Productivity changes.

H_{02}: Changes in Capital Expenditures are not related to Productivity changes.

H_{03}: Changes in Productivity are not related to Profitability changes.

H_{04}: Changes in Research and Development Expenses are not related to Profitability changes.

H_{05}: Changes in Capital Expenditures are not related to Profitability changes.

As shown in Figure 1, this study examines five relationships among four variables. Correlation analysis is used to assess the direction and strength of the relationships between various pairs of four variables (i.e., C_RD, C_CAP, Productivity, and C_ROA) in the study.

Since substantial investments are long-term in nature, increases in catalyst financial commitments may improve current and/or future performance (i.e., productivity and profitability results). If the input does not immediately affect the output in the same period, a time lag may exist. Such a lag is called delay or dead time because it delays the effect of input on output. In practice, some industries experience lags of more than a year, but published data concerning these time frames are not available. Howell and Soucy [NAA 1987] state that payback periods usually are less than three years in the new manufacturing environment. As a foundation for future studies, therefore, this study examine both one-year and two-year lags between changes in substantial investments and defined performance changes.

ASSUMPTIONS AND LIMITATIONS OF THE STUDY

This study operates on four primary assumptions. First, an assumption is made that the APC model for productivity measurement is generally applicable to all manufacturing companies. The APC productivity model, which provides an improved measure of changes in productivity, is based on gross profit. Second, an assumption is made that publicly available and accessible data can be as effective for this type of performance analysis as well as internally developed data. Third, this study assumes that the Producer Price Index published by the Department of Labor is appropriate for deflating measures of sales and cost of goods sold in each year of the study to the base year (i.e., 1980). Fourth, industries with capacity utilization rates above the average capacity utilization rate for its subgroup (nondurable or durable goods industries) are assumed to be more effective and efficient operating industries.

The study is limited in scope and methodology. In terms of scope, publicly available data are the sole source of information for analytical purposes. The sample for this study is limited to manufacturing industries and companies in the COMPUSTAT II files that satisfy all selection criteria for this study. Readers must thus be aware that the "industry construct" used for analysis purposes in this study does not include all companies that could be included in the various industry classifications. Therefore, conclusions drawn from the findings of this study represent operational phenomena only of industries and companies with substantial investments, and these results may not be applicable to other manufacturing environments. In addition, the time frame for this study is limited to the 1980-1989 period. Moreover, the investigation of time lags between substantial investments and resulting benefits is limited to the investment year and two succeeding years.

In terms of methodology, the APC model that is used to measure changes in productivity of the selected companies assumes a constant product mix between periods. In reality, a company may change its product mix because of competitive markets; however, information on such changes is not publicly available. This study is thus limited due to the lack of internal company information on the impacts of these product mix changes. Also important as a limitation is the fact that the management accounting literature provides no universally accepted method for developing inflation-adjusted measure of Return on Assets. For this reason, unadjusted return measures are used in this study.

ORGANIZATION OF THE STUDY

This study consists of six chapters. Chapter One introduces primary literature references, objectives of the study, research methodology, assumptions and limitations of the study. Chapter Two presents a review of the literature on productivity research, including studies on productivity measurement and factors contributing to productivity changes. Chapter Three presents a review of the management accounting literature relating to factors contributing to profitability changes. Chapter Four describes the research methodology in detail, including definitions, descriptions of models, sample selection procedures, research questions, and statistical analyses. Chapter Five is devoted to a summary of overall findings and results of all stages of data analyses. Chapter Six contains conclusions and recommendations based on analyses of the findings. The final chapter also includes suggestions for future research toward the application of productivity measurement models to other industries, companies, and countries.

II

Productivity Measurement Considerations

In the economics and management accounting literature productivity measurement is applied at national, industry, and company levels. This chapter reviews the relevant literature on productivity research at each of these three levels; ultimately, productivity measurements at industry and company levels are emphasized. Most studies in the economics literature have been focused on productivity measurement at the national level and/or industry level. Some studies in the management accounting literature discuss the application of productivity measurement at the company level.

Productivity, for macroeconomics purposes, is viewed generally as a measure of efficiency, the relationship between outputs and inputs for a total national economy (McInnes, 1984). Kendrick [1984] defines productivity at the micro level by using sales revenues as outputs and all production costs as inputs. Both definitions serve in this study as a general frame of reference for reviewing the relevant productivity literature.

THE U.S. FOCUS ON ECONOMIC GROWTH

Research on productivity at the national level is directly connected with an increased public interest in economic growth. One useful definition of economic growth is the steady process of increasing the productive capacity of the economy and, hence, of increasing national income (*The American Dictionary of Economics,* 1983). After the energy crisis of the 1970s, productivity research became even more important because of our need to achieve increased economic growth in the U.S. economy (Kendrick, 1984).

In the 1970s, the Committee on Changing International Realities of the National Planning Association appointed Dunn and Neftci as researchers to review recent American economic growth; they were to compare U.S. growth with the growth of six other major industrial countries, including Japan, the USSR, Canada, and three European countries (i.e., the United Kingdom, France, and West Germany). There were two major purposes for their study: (1) to evaluate the performance of the U.S. economy, and (2) to analyze the factors that could improve economic growth.

Dunn and Neftci [1980] found that economic growth in the 1970s was considerably less rapid than had been expected, and that the economy was plagued by combinations of inflation and high interest rates. Their findings can be verified by using the data of producer prices indexes and discount rates from the *Business Statistics* that are published by the U.S. Bureau of Economic Analysis. During the 1970s producer price indexes of all commodities were increasing, and by the end of the decade this "inflation" index was increasing by at least 9% annually. In the late 1970s the discount rate also jumped, from 7.46% in 1978 to 10.28% in 1979; interest rates were increasing dramatically as well.

The most common indicator used for evaluating the performance of an economy is the growth of real GNP per capita (Kendrick, 1977). Dunn and Neftci believe that GNP growth can be improved by many factor, such as a larger labor force and increased capital investment. Their comparison of U.S. GNP and U.S. labor productivity growth in the 1970s showed an interesting paradox. According to their empirical study, real GNP growth in that period continued and increased slightly even as labor productivity growth was declining sharply, This situation indicated that GNP growth was being influenced not only by labor productivity growth but also by other factors. Among these factors were changes in production methods and changes in capital investment which, together, may have outweighed the decline in labor productivity.

The Dunn and Neftci study suggests that economic growth can be increased by improvements in total factor productivity. In a related study, Gold [1979:29] notes: "Recent decades have been characterized by increasing acceptance of the belief that advances in productivity and technology constitute the most promising source of long-term gains in economic welfare." Given this reasoning, an inference that economic growth through productivity improvement may be stimulated by increases in research and development activities and capital expenditures seems reasonable.

CAPACITY UTILIZATION AT THE INDUSTRY LEVEL

The first comprehensive study of U.S. productivity at the industry level was done by Kendrick [1961]. His major contribution was to bring the research on productivity measurement from the national level to both manufacturing and non-manufacturing industry levels. In a later work, Kendrick [1984] states that chief factors in productivity improvement are the "cost-reducing" innovations in production processes.

Two economics studies employ capacity utilization measures in helping to evaluate the performance of capital investment (Berndt and Hesse, 1986; Lieberman, 1989). In the economics literature capacity utilization is usually defined as the ratio of actual output to the maximum potential output. Economics researchers use capacity utilization measures to assess both macroeconomic and micro-economic performance. At the macro level, Berndt and Hesse [1986] assess capacity utilization in the manufacturing industries of nine industrial countries (e.g., the United States, West Germany, and Japan) over the period 1960-1982. Empirical results of their study indicate that after 1973 (i.e., after the year of the energy crisis) excess capacity was pervasive and productivity decreased, with capacity utilization rates declining dramatically in the manufacturing sectors of nine industrial countries.

At the micro level, Lieberman [1989] assesses determinants of capacity utilization at the industry level and he views capacity utilization as a key determinant of corporate profitability. Although his study does not specify the industries investigated, the findings suggest that capacity utilization is positively related to capital investments. Lieberman also suggests that companies without a system for measuring their capacity utilization use the industrial capacity utilization rate for their industry as a surrogate.

MEASURING PRODUCTIVITY AT THE COMPANY LEVEL

The Davis [1955] study of productivity accounting is a first attempt to measure total factor productivity at the micro level. In the forward Kendrick describes Davis in the revised edition (1978) of *Productivity Accounting* as a pioneer in the development of the concept and measurement of what is now called "total factor productivity" at the company level. Davis recommends using productivity accounting to tell more about the efficient performance of a company and proposes a productivity statement that parallels the income statement and presents a productivity change as the difference between the ratio of output value to input costs in a base period and the ratio of output value to input costs in a given period. Output value (i.e., sales revenue) and input costs (i.e., cost of goods sold) for a given period are deflated to the base period value.

The Management Accounting Practices Committee of the NAA sponsored a series of research projects on productivity measurement in the late 1970s. Three articles reporting the results of these projects were published in 1980. Wait [1980] discusses the relationship between measurement at the national level and measurement at the company level. In addition, he also suggests an approach to applying productivity measurement at the company level. Mammone [1980a] reviews major studies on productivity research and includes a bibliography on this subject. Although the six companies are not manufacturing companies, Mammone [1980b] does present practical approaches to productivity measurement in case studies of six company settings.

Kaplan [1983] suggests using productivity measures as supplements to traditional financial measures of manufacturing performance. In his view, management accountants would separate variances due to relative price changes from those caused by changes in production efficiency. Belcher [1984] also supports integrating productivity measurement into the process of analyzing and interpreting financial data. He recommends using productivity measurement as an important element of the performance evaluation process.

ALTERNATIVE APPROACHES TO PRODUCTIVITY MEASUREMENT

In the economics literature productivity is usually defined as the ratio of output to input. Mundel [1983] defines productivity as a ratio of output produced per unit of resources consumed. Kendrick [1984] defines productivity as the ratio of output to inputs of labor and other resources, in real terms, at the company level. Sales revenues are used as this output measure, and all costs relating to the production of output, including inputs of material, labor, capital, and indirect business taxes, are measured as input costs. Productivity increases if the same output requires less input in the production process, or if the same input levels lead to increased output. Two distinct types of productivity ratios have been investigated in the literature, partial productivity ratios and total factor productivity ratios.

Partial Productivity

Partial productivity measures are derived by dividing total output by a single input. The early productivity researchers were mainly concerned with the changing status of labor. The partial productivity index of labor, which is a ratio of output divided by labor cost, was one of the first indexes of productivity. Belcher [1984] proposes partial productivity measures for four inputs — material, labor, capital, and energy — because these four factors are the major inputs for producing output. Kendrick [1984] states that a company may use partial productivity ratios if only one or two inputs are the major inputs in its production processes.

In fact, as noted in the next section where available models are discussed, partial productivity measures are criticized by many researchers. Belcher points out that one partial measure can be improved at the expense of another. For example, improvements in labor productivity may result from increases in capital investments. Mammone [1980a:37] thinks that a labor productivity index is unrealistic , stating that "the ratio of output to labor input may change for reasons unrelated to the quality of labor input." Craig and Harris [1973] comment that the cost of generating increased labor productivity must be considered in evaluating manufacturing performance. Generally speaking, partial productivity measures are useful in certain circumstances, but they have the serious shortcoming that substitutions among inputs may affect the resulting output measures.

Total Factor Productivity

Total factor productivity has been developed to remove the input substitution effects, and this construct is defined as total output divided by the sum of all the inputs. Solow [1957] developed an aggregate production function model that has become the basis of all subsequent studies in total factor productivity. Solow relates growth in his productivity index to a shift in the production function caused by technical improvements. Solow's framework, which is discussed in the next section, has created a great deal of interest in research on productivity improvement.

Total factor productivity is a measure of the relationship of revenues to manufacturing costs of all inputs at the company level (Kendrick, 1984). Labor is no longer the primary factor contributing to productivity improvement because other factors relating to the development of quality product and the installation of efficient equipment are often as important as labor inputs in the competitive marketplace. Consequently, total factor productivity is now thought to be the most effective measure of manufacturing performance in the new manufacturing environment (Kaplan,1983).

AVAILABLE PRODUCTIVITY MODELS

Six models for measuring total factor productivity are presented chronologically in this section. As early as 1928 Cobb and Douglas created a production function model. Readers should note that a difference exists between the terms productivity and production: productivity improvement means output increases without making additional inputs, whereas more inputs are needed to increase output in the production process (Nadler,1988). In the literature studies on production function moved toward productivity research after 1960. Solow [1957] developed an aggregate production function model that included technical changes as a variable. In the early 1970s, Craig and Harris created a different total productivity model. Three other productivity models—the NAA model, the APC model, and the PPP model—were also developed in the 1980s.

The Cobb-Douglas Production Function

The Cobb-Douglas production [1928] is a particular form of the general production function, $P = F(L,C)$, where P is production, L is labor, and C is capital. Relative to the index of production, the function of labor and capital in the 1928 Cobb-Douglas empirical study is as follows:

$$P' = b\,L^k C^{1-k}$$

where

$P' = $ Production index,

L = Labor,
C = Capital,
b and k = numerical values that make P' the best approximation of P
    in accordance with the Theory of Least Squares.

The Cobb-Douglas study is the first to recognize the importance of both labor and capital inputs to the production function. In their study, labor productivity is deemed to be more substantial than capital investment because of the labor intensity of the early 1900s. This production function is easy to understand and calculate. However, empirical analyses of this nature are difficult because required data can not be obtained directly from publicly available information (e.g., financial statements). In addition, this static model is of only limited usefulness because analyses do not consider the effects of substitutions among inputs in the production process.

The Solow Aggregate Production function

In order to avoid the possibility of input substitution effects, Solow [1957] developed an aggregate production function. The Solow model is as follows:

$$Q = F (K,L,t)$$

Q represents output, while K and L represent capital and labor inputs in "physical" units. The variable t for time appears in F to allow for technical changes.

Solow's study has led to major findings in productivity research. He found that the rate of productivity improvement for the economy as a whole was about one percent per year for the 1901-1917 period, approximately 1.2 percent per year for the 1918-1933 period, and about 1.6 percent per year from 1934 to 1949. His most surprising results show [1957:316] that "about one-eighth of the total increase is traceable to increased capital per man hour, and the remaining seven-eighths to technical changes." Most of Solow's work is aimed at explaining the productivity residual (i.e., technical changes).

In the Solow model the efficiency of the production process can be increased both by capital and labor inputs and by technical changes resulting in productivity improvements. Technical changes include advances in product quality and cost reduction. Data about specific technical changes and their impacts are not publicly available; thus, empirical applications of this model have not been forthcoming. As with the Cobb-Douglas model, data availability may be a problem for the Solow model.

The Craig and Harris Total Productivity Model

Craig and Harris [1973] created a simple model of total productivity. Their total productivity index is the ratio of output value to input costs, and all variables in the model are measured in dollars and deflated to a base period value. Output value is defined as the summation of all units produced times their selling price. Input costs are total costs for producing output. Labor input is the product of man hours and wage rate per hour. Capital input is the sum of depreciation expenses and maintenance expenses as obtained from the accounting records. Raw materials plus purchased parts make up total purchase costs. Other miscellaneous goods and services are comprised of all resources except for labor, capital, and raw materials. Their measure of total productivity at a company level is stated as follows:

$$P_t = O_t / (L+C+R+Q)$$

where

P_t = total productivity,
L = labor input factor,
C = capital input factor,
R = raw material and purchased parts input factor,
Q = other miscellaneous goods and services input factor,
O_t = total output.

Craig and Harris argue that all partial productivity measures have inherent fallacies and that productivity measurement should include all the factors related to production. Even though the concept of total factor productivity was created by Davis in 1955 and was also discussed by earlier researchers, the Craig and Harris work represents the most coherent and forceful case for total factor productivity measurement at the company level in the early 1970s. They [1973:15] emphasize that "to describe the calculation of total productivity for a company, a definition in dollars of all the above factors is required; and to make productivity indexes comparable from period to period, each index must be adjusted to a base period value."

The problem of productivity measurement as outlined by Craig and Harris thus lies in measuring trends. In their opinion, productivity in each period should be compared to a base period to determine increases or decreases in productivity. Therefore, all inputs and outputs in any period after the base period should be stated in the base-period dollar. They also recommend that the base period should be one in which no serious deviation from average production occurred.

The Craig and Harris model can be applied directly to observed data without statistical estimation of the underlying production structure; therefore, it is fairly understandable and reasonably easy to calculate. The possible restriction for the Craig and Harris model, however, is data availability, because material cost and labor cost normally do not appear on a company's audited financial statements.

The NAA Productivity Index Model

Most economics studies of productivity measurement are on the national scale, yet there is a need for productivity measurement at the company level. Corporate managers are concerned with productivity improvement because this measure offers a representative indicator of the overall efficiency of their companies. Therefore, in the late 1970s the Management Accounting Practices (MAP) Committee of the National Association of Accountants (NAA) developed a series of productivity measurement studies.

The productivity ratio is the ratio of output to input. In many manufacturing companies, labor is not now assumed to be a predominant resource because these companies install automated equipment for production processes. Consequently, for such operations materials, capital equipment, and other services are also important. In the NAA model, sales revenue means the product of selling price and units sold (selling price x units sold), and input costs are the manufacturing costs of four input elements: direct materials, employee compensation, facilities changes, and other services (Wait, 1980).

The NAA model is shown as follows:

Productivity ratio for current year PR(C) =
Sales adjusted to base year / Input costs adjusted to base year

Productivity ratio for the base year PR(B) =
Sales / Input costs

Productivity Index = PR(C)/ PR(B)

All the above variables are measured in dollars and can be obtained from a company's accounting system. The value of output and of each input is deflated by using the Consumer Price Index (CPI). The productivity index is a ratio of the productivity ratio for the current year to productivity ratio for the base year. The NAA productivity index is useful for a company that wishes to examines its own real growth. The limitation of this model is data availability because most companies don't provide the information on all input costs on an item by item basis in their financial reports. Thus, necessary analytical data can not be obtained from publicly available databases (e.g., COMPUSTAT).

The APC Productivity Model

The American Productivity Center (APC) performance measurement system includes three elements: profitability, productivity, and price recovery. Data required for the APC performance system are value, quantity, and price (value = quantity x price) for each output and input. The relationship between quantity of output and quantity of output and quantity of input is called "productivity." Output is defined as sales revenue and input is defined as cost of goods sold. Productivity is calculated "by subtracting each input change ratio from the total output change ratio and multiplying the resulting number by the input's value in period 1" (Belcher, 1984:44).

The APC productivity model uses a single-step deflation measurement approach. For example, if the base year is assumed to be 1980 and the current period is 1989, the deflated value of item X is its quantity in 1989 times its unit price in 1980.

The APC model is shown as follows:

$$\text{Productivity} = C_B \left[(S^D_t/S_B) - (C^D_t/C_B) \right]$$

where

C_B : Costs in the base period,

c^D_t : Costs in the period t deflated to the base period,

S_B : Sales in the base period,

S^D_t : Sales in period t deflated to the base period.

The APC model is gross-profit oriented and focuses on total factor productivity. In practice, gross profit is often used to evaluate manufacturing performance (Howell and Soucy, 1988). Table 2 shows the process of computing productivity using the APC model. Data are for the Control Data Corporation as recorded in the COMPUSTAT II files. Sales, cost of goods sold, and productivity are measured in millions of dollars. The base year is assumed to be 1980.

Table 2
The APC Productivity Model

Year	Sales	Cost of Goods Sold	Producer Price Index	Productivity
1980	2765.60	1664.40	100	0
1981	3101.30	1735.70	104.10	125.58
1982	4292.00	2143.50	108.10	406.59

$$1664.40 \ [(2765.60/2756.60) - (1664.40/1664.40)] = 0$$

$$1664.40 \ [(2982.02/2765.60) - (1668.94/1664.40)] = 125.58$$
$$3101.30 \times (100/104.10) = 2982.02$$
$$1735.70 \times (100/104.10) = 1668.94$$

$$1664.40 \ [(3970.40/2765.60) - (1982.89/1664.40)] = 406.59$$
$$4292.00 \times (100/108.10) = 3970.40$$
$$2143.50 \times (100/108.10) = 1982.89$$

The PPP Productivity Model

Ethyl Corporation's "Profitability = Productivity + Price recovery" (PPP) system is described clearly by Miller [1984]. Both the APC and the PPP systems have the same elements: profitability, productivity, and price recovery. Mathematically, the PPP productivity model is the same as the APC model.

The PPP model is described as follows:

$$\text{Productivity} = S_t^D \left[(S_t^D - C_t^D)/S_t^D - (S_B - C_B)/S_B \right]$$

where

C_B : Costs in the base period,

C_t^D : Costs in the period t deflated to the base period,

S_B : Sales in the base period,

S_t^D : Sales in period t deflated to the base period.

The major difference between the APC and PPP models, is the deflation method used in computing productivity (Miller and Rao, 1989). Instead of using a single-step deflation method, the PPP model uses a cumulative deflation method. The period-to-period price changes are chained together to produce a cumulative price deflator. Dividing a current period figure by the cumulative deflator allows the figure to be restated in the base year value (Miller, 1984). In contrast to the APC model, this deflating procedure may be too complicated for effective practical applications to occur. Perhaps for this reason the PPP model has not been broadly applied; to date, only the Ethyl Corporation has attempted its application in a practical setting (Miller and Rao, 1989).

Essentially, data availability is the major concern in the model selection process. The first four models surveyed in this chapter require internal company data, such as costs of labor and capital, physical units of output, and measures of capacity utilization. Due to problems associated with obtaining such data, these models are not used in this study to measure productivity. The APC and PPP models need only sales, cost of goods sold, and deflating factors; these data can be obtained from publicly available sources (e.g., COMPUSTAT). But the PPP deflating system is considerably more cumbersome than the APC's, the literature reveals that many manufacturing companies rely on the APC model (Kendrick 1984). Therefore, this study uses the APC productivity model to measure the productivity of the companies selected in the sample.

THE APC PERFORMANCE MEASUREMENT SYSTEM

The APC performance system is based on the actual quantities and prices of outputs and inputs over a period of time (Banker, Datar, and Kaplan, 1989). The APC system was developed by Carl Thor, Vice-president of the American Productivity Center (APC), which was organized in the late 1970s (Brayton, 1985). This system is derived from work initially done by the National Productivity Institute of the Republic of South Africa (Belcher, 1984). Essentially, the chief characteristic of this system is that profitability is defined as the function of productivity and price recovery. The key elements of the APC system (profitability = productivity x price recovery) are output and input measures. Both output and input are presented in terms of the following equation:

Value = Quantity x Price

In Figure 2, the APC performance measurement system is illustrated as a measure that distinguishes changes in profitability, productivity, and price recovery. Sourwine [1988:35] indicates, " This system results in a comparison of ratios and indices that can be converted into financial terms to explain resource utilization, pricing policies, and cost control." As Kendrick [1984:58] states, "The APC system is completely reconcilable with normal accounting systems."

Figure 2
The APC Performance System
Relationship Between Output and Input
-Values, Quantity, Price

OUTPUT VALUE	=	QUANTITY SOLD	x	UNIT PRICE
"Profitability"	=	"Productivity"	x	"Price recovery"
INPUT VALUE	=	QUANTITY USED	x	UNIT PRICE

The total dollar effects of both productivity and price recovery are used to explain changes in profit from one period to another (Kendrick, 1984). For output and input values, dollar values are determined by multiplying a physical quantity by unit price or unit cost. Output value is sales revenue and input value is cost of goods sold. The comparison between relative changes in values of outputs and inputs is the change in profitability. The relationship between quantities sold and quantities used in the second column, both at a given point in time and over time, is called productivity, an inflation-free measure of overall business performance (Kendrick, 1984). The third column in Figure 2, price recovery, is defined as the relationship between changes in unit prices and changes in unit costs over time, or the ability of an organization to pass through its unit cost changes in selling prices (Belcher, 1984).

Thor [1987] states that the APC performance measurement system is now used successfully by manufacturing and/or service sectors. In addition, this system can be most usually applied to analyze financial impacts of improving white collar productivity through investments in technical innovations (Thor, 1987; Belcher, 1984; Sourwine,1988). Data availability and simplicity are major factors underlying the popularity of the APC system. In general, necessary data can be derived from an company's financial statements.

Banker, Datar, and Kaplan [1989 indicate, however, that the APC system is not without shortcomings. They criticize the basic assumption of the APC system, a constant product mix between periods. In fact, a company can not keep the same product mix due to ongoing changes in the competitive market. Their study indicates that the APC system may signal productivity improvements even when there are no real improvements in the use of material, labor, and overhead. This "false" productivity improvement, they argue, is created only by the changes in the product mix. Furthermore, they point out that unrecognized fluctuations in the prices of outputs and inputs can distort a productivity measure.

FACTORS CONTRIBUTING TO PRODUCTIVITY IMPROVEMENT

Solow [1957] recognizes that changes in the production function can be related to technical improvements as well as capital and labor inputs. Kendrick [1984:52] agrees with Solow's observation and emphasizes, "The chief cause of productivity growth over the long run is a cost-reducing innovation in the technology and organization of production." McInnes [1984] empirically investigates factors contributing to productivity improvements in a sample of large industrial companies. His findings show that investments in research and development projects and capital outlays have positive effects on productivity improvements. During the last two decades, American businesses have faced inflation, high interest rates, and especially increasing international competition. To survive in the international marketplace, manufacturers have thus been forced to improve their production processes by increasing research and development expenses and capital expenditures to compete more effectively against low-cost, high-quality foreign competitors.

Effects of R&D Expenses

Economics studies discuss the relationships of investments in research and development activities, productivity improvements, and economic growth at the national level. Productivity improvements that result in economic growth are related to increased research and development activities. In his study, Solow [1957] points out that the unexplained difference in economic growth which can not be accounted for by changes in labor and capital inputs is the result of technological changes. Past economic studies suggest a number of specific relationships between research and development activities and economic growth, and also identify certain characteristics of the process of technological change to explain economic growth (Terleckyj, 1980). Rahman and Chowdhury [1988] find that changes in research and development activities affect economic growth through productivity improvement. They conducted a study to test for a causal relationship between changes in research and development activities and economic growth. They used three measures of productivity — National Income, National Income per person employed, National Income per hour of work in the nonresidential business sector — as the measurement of economic growth. Their findings show that this relationship is positive.

Impacts of Capital Expenditures

To compete in global markets, American companies must make substantially capital investments in automated facilities to improve their productivity. As Howell and Soucy [1988:4] point out, "Automation is probably the most visible change taking place in the new manufacturing environment." Findings in their field study show that many large U.S. manufacturers in the automotive, heavy equipment, and high technology industries (e.g., General Motors, GE, and IBM) have invested heavily in automated equipment to increase productivity in order to meet competitive challenges.

RELATIONSHIPS BETWEEN INVESTMENTS AND PRODUCTIVITY

The first part of this study is focused on the above two factors that contribute to improved productivity. The relationships between catalyst financial commitments and productivity are: (1) the effects of changes in Research and Development Expenses on Productivity changes and (2) the effects of changes in Capital Expenditures on Productivity changes as illustrated in the following:

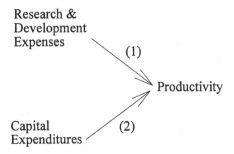

Benefits of these catalyst financial commitments may be realized in the current period or in future periods. In general, these increased investments may have positive (McInnes, 1984), negative (Gale,1980), or null (Morbey and Reithner, 1990) effects on current productivity. If these investments have negative or null effects on current productivity (Year 0) but positive effects on future productivity (Year 1 and/or Year 2), time lags between investment increases and productivity changes may exist. One of the research objectives of this study is to search for possible time lags.

Chapter Three deals with factors contributing to profitability changes. The literature on possible relationships between productivity changes and profitability changes is discussed therein. The effects of changes in research and development expenses and capital expenditures on changes in profitability are both discussed as well. Finally, the literature on possible time lags between catalyst financial commitments and profitability changes is explored. Together, additional information about these types of relationships should assist management accountants in their efforts to develop improved planning and control models.

III

Productivity,
Catalyst Commitments,
and Profitability

In an environment of global competition, manufacturing companies must produce better quality goods at lower costs to maintain their customer bases (Howell and Soucy, 1988; Kaplan 1983). Many American manufacturers have thus been forced to increase their research and development expenses to improve product quality and to increase capital expenditures to reduce product costs in order to survive in international markets. Productivity measurement and the effects of these catalyst commitments on productivity changes were discussed in Chapter Two. Since productivity improvements and profitability growth are fundamental to a company's survival, relationships between catalyst commitments and both of these factors are also most relevant.

The first part of the current chapter reviews the literature on the possible effects of productivity improvements on profitability changes. Many studies have looked at the relationship between productivity and profitability. The primary studies of interest in this context are the National Association of Accountants (NAA) studies and the studies using the American Productivity Center (APC) performance measurement system. Together, these studies show that profitability is influenced by several factors and that productivity improvements are important considerations as managers attempt to achieve increases in profitability.

The second part of this chapter discusses the literature on direct impacts of catalyst financial commitments (i.e., Research and Development Expenses and Capital Expenditures) on profitability. In the manufacturing industries, large companies strongly support research and development projects to create both new and improved products (Kendrick, 1984). In addition, American manufacturers increase their capital investments in order to gain added efficiencies in their production processes. Automation is having positive impacts by reducing the need for expensive labor in the new manufacturing environment (Howell and Soucy,1988). Production lines are more flexible and thus cost-reducing by nature. For these reasons, increased research and development expenses and capital expenditures are viewed as having dramatic impacts on U.S. profitability.

Once these relationships are determined, there remains the question of timing of investment impacts. The literature on possible time lags between changed catalyst financial commitments and productivity/profitability changes is also discussed in this chapter. Together, these variables should comprise the substance of improved planning and control models as management accountants work toward financial improvements in the new manufacturing environment.

The DuPont model of profitability analysis, Return on Investment, is widely known in the management accounting literature. This measure, termed Return on Assets in this study, can be divided into two ratios: profit margin and asset turnover. Johnson and Kaplan [1987] state that the DuPont model provides an excellent example of the early uses of management accounting to evaluate profitability in a company.

PRODUCTIVITY AND PROFITABILITY

Empirical studies of the relationship between productivity improvement and profitability change are limited (McInnes, 1984). In the early 1980s, three studies on productivity measurement (Wait, 1980; Mammone, 1980a, 1980b) were sponsored by the Management Accounting Practices Committee of the National Association of Accountants (NAA). Other studies (Kendrick, 1984; Belcher, 1984; Brayton, 1985) in the mid-1980s discussed the American Productivity Center performance measurement system that connects changes in profitability, productivity and price recovery. Findings from these efforts suggest several ways to approach the productivity/profitability relationship in the U.S. manufacturing sector. However, none of these previous works have attempted to investigate these critical relationships by using easily accessible and publicly available databases.

NAA Productivity Studies

Wait [1980] focuses on productivity measurement at the company level. He identifies productivity as a physical measure and profitability as a financial measure, and notes that changes in productivity affect profitability. As Wait [1980:27] indicates, "Changes in productivity are a basic determinant of changes in costs, in productive capacity and of the potential benefits of changes in product mix-all bearing significantly on enterprise profitability." For a manufacturer, productivity improvements result in good quality products and high capacity utilization. Product prices can be increased because of good quality, and unit costs can be reduced because more units are produced without increasing manufacturing costs. Wait uses data from a hypothetical company to calculate two-year productivity ratios using the NAA productivity index. This productivity index is a ratio of the productivity ratio for the current year to the productivity ratio for the base year. The productivity ratio is a ratio of sales revenue to manufacturing costs. The results of this case study show that productivity improvement is correlated with profitability growth.

Like Wait, Mammone [1980a] points out that productivity improvements have effects on changes in profitability. To assist management in understanding productivity measurement, he reviews the authoritative research on this subject. In the first of two studies for the NAA, Mammone [1980a:36] states that "improved productivity would result in greater profits for management through greater output at reduced costs." He criticizes partial productivity measurement, pointing out that investments in new equipment may improve labor productivity while total factor productivity actually declines.

Mammone [1980b] presents the results of a field survey conducted by the NAA researchers. This study discusses the application of the NAA productivity index to six companies (e.g., metal producer, equipment manufacturer, food processor, and three non-manufacturing companies). For each case, the index is expressed as the ratio of output to input in physical units or in dollars, but what comprises input costs varies depending on the industry. Even through this study does not focus directly on manufacturing companies, Mammone suggests an integration of accounting and productivity measurement concepts. He argues that the productivity measurement system can be used to explain the variances between budgeted and actual operating results that are shown in financial statements.

Studies Using the APC System

Two studies suggest using the APC system as a measure of manufacturing performance (Kendrick, 1984; Belcher, 1984). As discussed in Chapter Two, the premise of this system is that profitability is generated from two sources: productivity and price recovery. Basically, the APC system shows a multiplier relationship in which profitability is the product of productivity and price recovery. In this system, factors contributing to profitability increases can be productivity improvements and/or inflation effects.

Kendrick [1984] states that a major factor in profitability increases is productivity improvement. This implies that productivity improvement is fundamental to profitability growth in competitive markets. He thinks of productivity improvements as a result of "cost-reducing innovations in the technology and organization of production" (Kendrick, 1984:52). These innovations result from investments in research and development projects and improved equipment (e.g., automation).

Belcher [1984] suggests that productivity may be the only weapon to offset the effects of inflation on profitability. He states [1984:4] that "changes in profitability result, in a broad sense, from just two factors: productivity (the effectiveness with which we utilize all of our resources) and price recovery (the relative changes in selling prices and unit costs of input)." Belcher emphasizes that the better way to increase profitability is to improve productivity over the long run. In contrast, a company that tries to offset declining productivity by raising its selling prices more than is required by increases in input costs will become uncompetitive in the long term.

CATALYST FINANCIAL COMMITMENTS AND PROFITABILITY

The Howell and Soucy study [1988] emphasizes the need for higher quality products with lower costs if American companies are to cope effectively with increasing competition in both domestic and international markets. Companies may improve product quality through technological innovations that result from investments in research and development, or they may increase their capital expenditures (e.g., automation) so that their production processes become more efficient. Good quality products can increase sales revenues, and efficient production processes can reduce product costs. Consequently, profits increase as a result of higher revenues and lower costs.

The previous discussion has dealt with the impacts of productivity improvements on profitability growth. However, catalyst financial commitments (i.e., Research and Development Expenses and Capital Expenditures) may also have direct effects on profitability. These direct effects are discussed immediately below.

Increased Research and Development Expenses

Manufacturing companies invest in research and development to create better products and/or reduce product costs. In the automobile industry, for example, companies are being forced to improve product quality and reduce product costs because of tough competition in the marketplaces. Howell and Soucy [1988:2] state that "quality is not expense, nonquality is" and quote a statement from Harold K. Sperlich, president of Chrysler: "To put value into the marketplace and meet the competitive challenge, you have to run a cost-effective business dedicated to constant, never-ending improvement." They emphasize that product quality is a major factor for successful businesses.

Gold [1979] suggests that the contributions of research and development expenses to profitability can be measured in the form of increased revenues and reduced costs. He discusses two hypothetical scenarios for the impact of increases in research and development expenses on profitability changes. The first scenario would be typical of companies making generic products. When all competitors make equal commitments to research and development projects, have the same targets, and are equally successful on average, there may be no consistent competitive advantage to any company even if all competitors increase their commitments; sometimes one and sometimes another would reach the goal first.

In the second scenario, one company makes a higher commitment to research and development expenses than its competitors in order to produce new of unique products. That company may improve profitability through technological innovations that result in revenue increases and cost reductions. In general, better quality should attract more customers and lower cost should offer competitive advantages.

Increased Capital Expenditures

Howell and Soucy [1988] focus on increased automation as one of the major changes in the new manufacturing environment. Many companies, particularly in the automobile and computer industries, have been forced to install energy-efficient equipment to increase manufacturing flexibility and reduce costs. Since such investment in capital improvements are substantial, American manufacturers are now evaluating more fully the benefits of advanced manufacturing technology. For these manufacturing companies, investments in automated facilities are expected to reduce production costs and then to increase profits.

The management accounting literature includes many studies of cases of successful automation in manufacturing industries, primarily in the automobile and electronics industries. For example, General Motors and Ford installed automated facilities in order to compete in the global market (Howell and Soucy, 1988). In the electronics industry, many companies have automated processes in their factories, such as automated equipment for Apple Computer and an automated final assembly and test module at IBM Lexington (Howell and Soucy, 1988).

Howell and Soucy [1988] also argue that traditional investment analyses focusing primarily on direct cost saving from labor, scrap, and inventory are not appropriate for evaluating investments in the new manufacturing environment. With high investment in automated production equipment, labor cost is often reduced rapidly. They state that benefits associated with advanced automation include quality, delivery, throughput, and flexibility, as well as cost savings resulting from advanced automation. These benefits may have direct and indirect impacts on profitability.

Gale [1980] and Ghemawat and Caves [1986] are both empirical studies that investigate the effect of capital investment on profitability. Although these two studies do not specify the industries investigated, both show that capital investment plays an important role in profitability growth. Capital investment leads to a higher production level, and unit costs are reduced because fixed costs are allocated over a larger volume of output.

These two studies use the Profit Impact of Market Strategy (PIMS) database, which is compiled by the Strategic Planning Institute (SPI). The population of the PIMS database includes more than 200 manufacturing and service companies of all sizes located in North America, Europe, and Australia. Most of the information in this database relates to factors that affect profitability growth. Gale [1980:80] states that the PIMS database contains "the data over 200 separate characteristics of each business experience, not only traditional balance sheet and income statement data but also information about market share, investment intensity, capacity utilization, product quality, and unionization."

Most variables in the PIMS database are related to factors that contribute to profitability changes, including gross profit rates, a ratio of research and development expenses to revenue, capacity utilization rate, etc. The PIMS database can be useful for empirical studies on profitability and can be accessed on a fee basis. The major limitation of the PIMS is that data in the database can not be verified by using other sources (e.g., annual reports). In contrast, the database for this study is the COMPUSTAT II files; these can easily be checked to insure the accuracy of data used for productivity and profitability measurement processes.

PROFITABILITY GROWTH AND TIME LAGS

Theoretically, profitability can be increased by productivity improvements that result from technological innovations and cost-reducing processes. However, managers should not expect that productivity improvement and substantial investments in research and development and capital expenditures necessarily affect profitability in the current period. Gold [1979] suggests that technological innovations that improve product quality may not immediately increase profitability; instead, the effects may be realized over long time periods. His suggestion points to the possible existence of time lags between investments in research and development and profitability. In addition, he states that increased investments may actually reduce short-term profitability. The expected benefits from technological innovation tend to be delayed during the early periods because of the need to effectively integrate adjustments in labor tasks and skills.

Gale [1980] additionally notes that in some circumstances increased capital investments actually reduce short-term profitability. In fact, investments in Capital Expenditures may have negative or null effects on current profitability (Gale, 1980; McInnes,1984). Thus, expected profitability improvements may not be realized until new facilities reach reasonably high levels of utilization. Discernible time lags between capital investments (e.g., automation) and profitability changes exist in some industries because such investments often need long implementation periods. Alternatively, capital investments may improve current productivity but have no effect on current profitability when the expected benefits from productivity improvements are delayed during the early period. As a result, increased capital intensity may affect profitability only over the long run.

Howell and Soucy [1988] suggest that time lags exist between substantial investments and performance changes because financial commitments for advanced automation purposes are more expensive, longer term, and more risky. They use two examples that show differences in time lags. General Motors' Saturn project, for instance, was expected to require five years before it was ready for production. In contrast, Allen-Bradley took only two years to implement fully its "world-wide" contractor facility. In this study, the investigation of time lags between substantial investments and resulting benefits is limited to the year of increases in investments and two succeeding years.

Prior studies on the five relationships and the existence of possible time lags were discussed in Chapter Two and above in this chapter. Each study discusses only one or two relationships among the four variables in this study. The Gold [1955] managerial control ratios model demonstrates possible relationships between profitability and several other factors. His model, which is used as a foundation for this study, is discussed in the following section.

THE GOLD MANAGERIAL CONTROL RATIOS MODEL

Return on Investment analysis (i.e., the DuPont model) is an important management accounting measure that can be used to evaluate the relative profitability of a company or an operating unit. In his 1955 study Gold developed a basic model of managerial control ratios and decomposed aggregate performance criteria into their component determinants. In the Gold model, changes in the ratio of profit to total investment are attributed to five areas of performance as follow:

Figure 3
The Gold Model

$$\frac{\text{Profit}}{\text{Total Investment}} = \left(\frac{\text{Product Value}}{\text{Output}} - \frac{\text{Total Cost}}{\text{Output}} \right)$$

$$\times \frac{\text{Output}}{\text{Capacity}} \times \frac{\text{Capacity}}{\text{Fixed Investment}} \times \frac{\text{Fixed Investment}}{\text{Total Investment}}$$

The five areas of performance are : product prices (total product value/output), unit costs (total costs/output), facilities utilization (output/capacity), productivity of facilities and equipment (capacity/fixed investment), and the allocation of investment resources between capital goods and working capital (fixed investment/total investment). Both facilities utilization and productivity of facilities are measured in physical units. The other three ratios are derived from analyses of financial data (Gold and Kraus, 1964).

Changes in the rate of profit on total investment are influenced by the interactions of changes in the five factors. According to Gold's model, efforts to increase the rate of profit on total investment need not involve concentration on quality-improvement innovations alone. On the contrary, Gold recognizes explicitly that Return on Investment may also be increased by price increases and the reduction of unit costs. As product quality improves, therefore, product prices can often be increased. Basically, investments in research and development projects can lead to technological innovations that improve product quality. Furthermore, investments in fixed assets (i.e., capital investments) can contribute to cost-reducing production processes.

Gold notes that the rate of profit to total investment can be affected by productivity improvements directly and indirectly. In the Gold model, profitability growth is related to changes in productivity (e.g., increases in the output levels of products exceed increases in resource inputs). For manufacturers, productivity improvements may result from both new and/or improved production designs and higher levels of capacity utilization. Production designs can be improved by increasing research and development expenses. Capacity utilization rates can be changed by increasing capital investments for new facilities. Productivity improvements can have direct effects on unit costs; then price output may also be affected (Gold, 1955). Consequently, the rate of profit to total investment can be positively improved by increases in product prices, fixed investments, productivity, and capacity utilization, or by decreases in unit costs.

Based on the Gold studies [1955; 1964; 1980], the relationships among the variables in the Gold model are summarized in the following diagram.

Figure 4
Major Relationships in the Gold Model

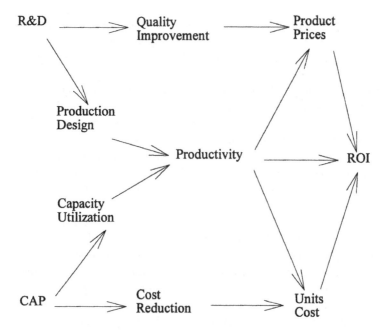

As shown in Figure 4, changes in research and development expenses and changes in capital expenditures may have effects on both productivity and profitability, and improved productivity can affect profitability directly and indirectly.

Data availability may be the major problem in using the Gold model in empirical studies. His model requires internal company data (e.g., capacity utilization) that usually can not be obtained from publicly available sources (e.g., financial statements). In any case, most manufacturing companies do not even have a means of measuring capacity. In addition, the productivity index in his model is defined as a ratio of capacity to fixed investment without a consideration of material and labor inputs. Therefore, this productivity index may be most suitable for a capital-intensive company where the costs of these two inputs are minor compared with the depreciation expenses of facilities in the production processes. Nevertheless, his managerial control ratios model can assist management accountants in planning, controlling, and evaluating operating performance by providing insight into the sources of changes in operating costs and revenues (Mammone, 1980a). In connection with the current study, the reader should note that if six variables (i.e., production design, capacity utilization, quality improvement, cost reduction, product prices, and unit costs) are eliminated from the above diagram, Figure 4 becomes identical to the Study Focus Model.

SUMMARY OBSERVATIONS ON PROFITABILITY GROWTH

The dominant issues for the corporation are those directly associated with survival and success-productivity and profitability. Increasing levels of international competition have forced American manufacturers to cut costs, raise productivity, and provide high quality goods to satisfy customer needs. To explain the effects of productivity on overall performance, Wait [1980] notes that improvement in productivity by each individual enterprise is necessary for it to remain competitive and to improve its profitability. Kendrick [1984] also notes that productivity is fundamental to profitability. Furthermore, the relevant literature reveals that increased catalyst financial commitments (i.e., research and development projects and capital improvements) can have direct effects on profitability when they lead to innovations in technology or expanded capacity and more efficient facilities. The following diagram presents these three relationships.

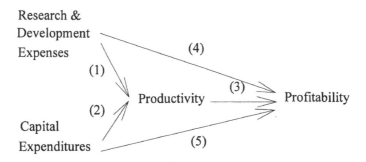

In summary, three relationships are examined in this chapter and two other relationships were discussed in the previous chapter. Because substantial investments in research and development and capital expenditures may affect current and/or future performance, the possibility of time lags between changes in these investment and changes in productivity and profitability is also introduced in these two chapters. At the end of this chapter, the Gold managerial control ratios model is presented as the theoretical foundation for the five relationships in this study.

IV

Research and Methodology

Throughout the past quarter-century U.S. businesses have confronted difficult economic conditions (i.e., increasing inflation and high interest rates) and increasing international competition as well. These higher levels of competitiveness have forced U.S. manufacturers to improve product quality while reducing costs. The resulting emphasis on productivity improvement and profitability growth is now considered to be essential for survival in the international marketplace.

Many U.S. manufacturing companies have made rapid changes in recent years to meet global competition. Improved quality and more cost-effective production processes are two of the major changes that have occurred (Howell and Soucy, 1988). Major improvements in product quality are being achieved through increased research and development outlays, and necessary automation requires substantial investments in capital improvements. Together, these increased catalyst financial commitments are usually assumed to have had impacts on productivity and/or profitability.

To date, however, empirical studies have not focused directly on these critical variables and relationships. Also relevant, the literature does not reveal any prior efforts to use publicly available data for these analytical purposes. This study addresses both needs as a basis for planning and control efforts by practicing management accountants.

THE ANALYTICAL MODEL

This study focuses directly on factors thought to contribute to advances in American manufacturing industries. Four critical variables (i.e., C_RD, C_CAP, Productivity, and C_ROA) and relationships between them are examined. To illustrate these relationships, Figure 5 is revisited here.

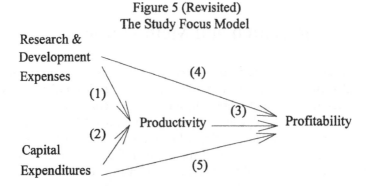

Figure 5 (Revisited)
The Study Focus Model

As was discussed in Chapters Two and Three, the literature reveals that increases in research and development expenses and capital expenditures ·can lead to improvements in productivity and/or profitability.

Research Hypotheses

As shown in Figure 1, the Study Focus Model presents five major relationships among four variables. Based on these relationships, five hypotheses are to be tested in each subgroup (e.g., industry and company) of this study as follows:

H_{01}: Changes in Research and Development Expenses are not related to Productivity changes.

H_{02}: Changes in Capital Expenditures are not related to Productivity changes.

H_{03}: Productivity changes are not related to Profitability changes.

H_{04}: Changes in Research and Development Expenses are not related to Profitability changes.

H_{05}: Changes in Capital Expenditures are not related to Profitability changes.

Definitions and Measures of Variables

The following definitions and measures of variables are utilized throughout this study. The definitions of Research and Development Expenses and Capital Expenditures are taken from the manual of COMPUSTAT. Definitions of productivity and profitability are drawn from other studies. Measurement of each variable is explained in detail. Productivity in dollars is calculated using the APC productivity model; specifically, this key measure presents monetary measures compared to the base year. The other three variables are also measured as changes compared to the base year.

Research and Development Expenses. Changes in Research and Development Expenses are measured in percentages as increases in these expenses are compared to the base year. In the COMPUSTAT manual Research and Development Expenses are defined as all research costs incurred during the year that relate to the development of new products or services. The figures from COMPUSTAT do not indicate which companies continued to amortize pre-1975 research and development costs into the early 1980s. However, the amounts of any such amortization would not be material to the results of this study. Changes in Research and Development Expenses (C_RD) are measured as follows:

C_RD(%) = (Current R&D - Base Year R&D)/ Base Year R&D.

The change in Research and Development Expenses for the current year is computed by dividing the difference between current-year expenses and base-year expenses by the base-year expenses by the base-year Research and Development Expenses.

Capital Expenditures. Changes in Capital Expenditures are measured in percentages as increases in Capital Expenditures compared to the base year. In the COMPUSTAT manual Capital Expenditures are the dollars spent on the construction and acquisition of property, plant, and equipment in a given year. Changes in Capital Expenditures (C_CAP) are measured in the following:

C_CAP(%) = (Current Cap Exp - Base Cap Exp) / Base Cap Exp.

The change in Capital Expenditures for the current year is computed by dividing the difference between current-year expenditures and base-year expenditures by the base-year Capital Expenditures.

Productivity. This study follows Kendrick's definition of total factor productivity, that is, the ratio of outputs to inputs of labor and other resources. The APC productivity model is used to measure productivity value in dollars. Productivity is calculated in the following:

$$\text{Productivity} = C_B \left[(S^D_t / S_B) - (C^D_t / C_B) \right]$$

where

C_B : Costs in the base period,

C^D_t : Costs in the period t deflated to the base period,

S_B : Sales in the base period,

S^D_t : Sales in period t deflated to the base period.

Productivity is calculated by subtracting each input change ratio from the output change ratio and then multiplying the result by the input value in the base year. Input value means cost of goods sold and output value means sales revenue.

The APC productivity model uses a single-step deflation method that has only one base year. For example, if the base year is assumed to be 1980 and the time frame for the research is the 1980-1989 period, all the values in these ten years are deflated to the 1980 values.

Producer price indexes are used as deflators. These indexes for major industries are published by the Department of Commerce. Based on the Standard Industrial Classification (SIC) codes, each industry has a producer price index for each year, which is used to deflate the figures for sales and cost of goods sold in each year. If there is no producer price index for an industry, the producer price index of the most similar industry is used as a surrogate. For example, the producer price index of the paper mills industry (SIC=2621) is used for two similar industries, paper and allied products (SIC=2600) and paperboard (SIC=2670).

Profitability. Changes in Return on Assets are measured in percentages as increases in profitability compared to the base year. The ratio of Return on Assets (i.e., the DuPont model) is the dominant measure of profitability in the management accounting literature. In this study, Return on Assets is defined as the ratio of net operating income to total assets. Net operating income is the amount of income before extraordinary items in COMPUSTAT II. Changes in Return on Assets (C_ROA) are computed as follows:

C_ROA(%) = (Current ROA - Base Year ROA) / Base Year ROA.

The change in Return on Assets for the current year is computed by dividing the difference between the current-year ratio and the base-year ratio by the base-year Return on Assets.

Description of COMPUSTAT

The COMPUSTAT II files contain financial data for 2,478 companies in 382 industries. The primary sources of this database are the 10K (Annual) and 10Q (Quarterly) reports to the Securities and Exchange Commission (SEC), and the reporting companies annual and quarterly reports. Since COMPUSTAT is updated annually, this uses annual data in its analyses.

Data needed to compute the four critical variables of this study (i.e., C_RD, C_CAP, Productivity, and C_ROA) are described in the following:

Figure 6
Data Source

Data in COMPUSTAT	Variable
Research and Development Expenses	C_RD
Capital Expenditures	C_CAP
Sales	Productivity
Cost of Goods Sold	Productivity
Income Before Extraordinary Items	C_ROA
Total Assets	C_ROA

Research and Development Expenses are used to compute C_RD. Capital Expenditures are applied to measure C_CAP. Sales and cost of goods sold are used to compute Productivity. Then, income before extraordinary items is combined with total assets to calculate C_ROA.

The four measured variables are illustrated in Table 3 by using data from the Control Data Corporation. The variables taken directly from the COMPUSTAT II files are Research and Development Expenses (R&D), Capital Expenditures (CAPITAL), sales (SALE), cost of goods sold (COST), income before extraordinary items (INCOME), and total assets (ASSET). In COMPUSTAT the "income before extraordinary items" figure is the net operating income from the income statement, and the amount of the "total assets" is the bottom line figure from the balance sheet. The producer price index, used for deflating figures to base-year values, is published by the Department of Labor. Other variables (e.g., C_RD, C_CAP, Productivity, and C_ROA) are computed.

STUDY STRATEGY

The study investigates relationships between changes in catalyst financial commitments and specified performance changes (i.e., changes in productivity and profitability). The overall strategy for the sample selection is to choose a period with productivity improvement in the U.S. manufacturing sector and to select companies with substantial investments in both research and development and capital expenditures. All selection criteria are discussed in this section. Time lag considerations are discussed as well.

Table 3
Control Data Corporation Data Set

Year	RD*	C_RD	C_RD1	C_RD2	INCOME*	ASSET*
1980	182.80	•	•	•	147.80	2534.80
1981	201.90	0.10	•	•	169.80	2825.90
1982	220.50	0.21	0.10	•	155.10	6911.88
1983	270.70	0.48	0.21	0.10	61.70	8777.57
1984	300.30	0.64	0.48	0.21	5.10	9573.50
1985	316.10	0.73	0.64	0.48	-530.60	3072.50
1986	313.90	0.72	0.73	0.64	-268.50	2594.90
1987	322.80	0.77	0.72	0.73	25.00	2638.60
1988	335.70	0.84	0.77	0.72	1.70	2533.50
1989	249.90	0.37	0.84	0.77	-680.40	1860.70

Table 3 (Continued)
Control Data Corporation Data Set

Year	CAPITAL*	C_CAP	C_CAP1	C_CAP2	ROA	C_ROA
1980	408.80	•	•	•	0.06	•
1981	270.60	-0.34	•	•	0.06	0.03
1982	260.70	-0.36	-0.34	•	0.02	-0.62
1983	257.40	-0.37	-0.36	-0.34	0.02	-0.68
1984	203.00	-0.50	-0.37	-0.36	0.00	-0.99
1985	160.30	-0.61	-0.50	-0.37	-0.17	-3.96
1986	156.70	-0.62	-0.61	-0.50	-0.10	-2.77
1987	178.30	-0.56	-0.62	-0.61	0.01	-0.84
1988	256.90	-0.37	-0.56	-0.62	0.00	-0.99
1989	156.40	-0.62	-0.37	-0.56	-0.37	-7.27

Year	Sale*	Cost*	PRI	Product*	Product1*	Product2*
1980	2765.60	1664.40	100.00	•	•	•
1981	3101.30	1735.70	104.10	125.58	•	•
1982	4292.00	2143.50	108.10	406.59	125.58	•
1983	4582.78	2329.70	110.90	386.22	406.59	125.58
1984	5026.90	2570.50	116.10	391.73	386.22	406.59
1985	3679.70	2373.50	119.90	-132.59	391.73	386.22
1986	3346.70	2063.70	119.30	-41.56	-132.59	391.73
1987	3366.50	2130.20	121.10	-86.02	-41.56	-132.59
1988	3628.30	2329.50	124.90	-116.80	-86.02	-41.56
1989	2934.50	1894.80	125.10	-102.92	-116.82	-86.02

Notes: The asterisk(*) indicates the amount in millions of dollars.

The six variables taken from COMPUSTAT II are RD, CAPITAL, SALE, COST, INCOME, and ASSET. PPI denotes the Producer Price Index. Other variables are computed

Time Frame Consideration

The time frame for this study is the ten-year period 1980-1989. Three major reasons support the selection of this time frame: (1) data availability, (2) manufacturing productivity improvements, and (3) the 1974 accounting standard change. The COMPUSTAT II files are used as the database for this research. This tape contains financial data, including items from income statements, balance sheets, statements of changes in financial positions, and market information for the 20 years 1970-1989. At the time this study was undertaken, the most current data in COMPUSTAT were for 1989. Table 1 (Chapter One) shows that total factor productivity in the manufacturing sector outpaced that of the overall business economy in the 1980s. Because this study focuses largely on relationships between changes in catalyst financial commitments and the specified performance changes, the time frame chosen was from 1980 to 1989. Productivity was regularly increasing in the manufacturing sector in that decade.

Also important is that this time frame comes after the issuance of Statement of Financial Accounting Standard No.2, Accounting for Research and Development Costs, effective for fiscal years beginning on or after January 1, 1975. That statement required that research and development costs be charged to expenses when incurred. Any impact this accounting change may have had upon management' decisions with respect to investments in research and development projects should be mitigated in the 1980-1980 period.

Industry Selection Criteria

Five major relationships are tested in this study. The scope of the study is limited to companies with substantial investments in both research and development and capital improvements. If a manufacturing company spends more than $1 million annually on advanced technology, the amount of its investments is considered substantial (Howell and Soucy, 1988). To choose companies with substantial investments, both industry and company selection criteria are used.

Four industry selection criteria are used in the selection of the sample for this study: (1) type of industry, (2) annual amount of Research and Development Expenses, (3) annual amount of Capital Expenditures, and (4) capacity utilization rate. Each selection criterion is detailed below.

Type of Industry. This research emphasizes empirical analysis of the relationships between increased catalyst financial commitments and performance changes in the U.S. manufacturing sector. Therefore, only manufacturing industries are included in this study. According to the U.S. Department of Commerce system, industries with the first two digits of their Standard Industrial Classification (SIC) codes in the range of 20-39 are defined as manufacturing industries. All the manufacturing industries are classified into two subcategories: nondurable goods and durable goods. The nondurable industries are these industries for which the first two digits of the SIC codes are 20-23 and 26-31; the durable industries are those for which the first two digits of the SIC codes are 24, 25, and 32-39. Each industry has a SIC code. One sector includes all similar industries of which the first two digits of their SIC codes are the same numbers. For example, the pharmaceutical preparations industry (SIC=2834) is in the chemicals sector (SIC=28).

Annual Amount of R&D Expenses. Manufacturing industries that invest substantial amounts in research and development projects are included in the sample. About 20% of the 382 industries in the population of COMPUSTAT II have average annual research and development expenses in excess of $10 million. The average annual amount of $10 million is used as the industry selection criterion. To be included in the sample, the average annual research and development expenses of each manufacturing industry for the ten-year period 1980-1989 should be greater than $10 million.

Annual Amount of Capital Expenditures. Only manufacturing industries that have substantial investments in capital expenditures are included in the sample. In the population of COMPUSTAT II, about 60% of the 382 industries have average annual capital expenditures of more than $10 million. The average annual amount of $10 million is also used as the criterion for capital expenditures. For each selected industry, the mean of annual capital expenditures for the 1980-1989 period should be greater than $10 million.

Capacity Utilization Rate. This study is interested in manufacturing industries with efficient production processes. An industry with above average capacity utilization rate is assumed to have efficient operations. To be included in the sample, an industry must have a capacity utilization rate that is greater than the average annual capacity utilization rate for its subgroup (nondurable or durable goods industries). The practical rate of capacity utilization, as published in the *Survey of Plant Capacity,* is the source for this information. The practical rate of capacity utilization is the value of actual output divided by the value of practical output. The latter measure is defined as the greatest output that a plant can achieve within the framework of realistic work patterns.

The average annual capacity utilization rates for both nondurable and durable industries are shown in Table 4. Because the *Survey of Plant Capacity* is completed only every five years, the most current year for capacity utilization rates is 1987. Therefore, the mean capacity utiliza-tion rates for the eight-year period 1980-1987—73% for nondurable goods and 63% for durable goods industries—are used as the basis for industry selection. If there is no capacity utilization rate for a given industry, the capacity utilization rate of the most similar industry is used as a surrogate. For example, the capacity utilization rate of the computer and office equipment industry is used for the electronic computers industry.

Table 4
Capacity Utilization Rates (%)
(Practical Rate)

Year	Nondurable Industries (SIC=20-23,26-31)	Durable Industries (SIC=24,25,32-39)
1980	76	65
1981	72	63
1982	69	53
1983	73	61
1984	72	65
1985	72	65
1986	73	64
1987	74	67
Average CU Rate	78	63

* Source : Bureau of the Census, U.S. Department of Commerce.

Selected industries must satisfy all four industry selection criteria in sequence. The manufacturing industries that are included in the study all have substantial investments in both research and development and capital expenditures and the mean of annual capacity utilization rates above those of their subgroups.

Company Selection Criteria

The four company selection criteria are : (1) annual amount of Research and Development Expenses, (2) annual amount of Capital Expenditures, (3) availability of complete 10-year data, and (4) no change in inventory valuation methods during the 1980-1989 period. Each criterion is discussed below.

Annual Amount of R&D Expenses. After specific manufacturing industries have been selected, only companies within each industry that report substantial research and development expenses are selected in the sample. In the population for the 1980-1989 period, about 20% of the 2478 companies have mean research and development expenses greater than $1 million per year. The mean amount of $1 million annually is used as the company selection criterion. For the selected companies mean research and development expenses for the ten-year period 1980-1989 are greater than $1 million per year.

Annual Amount of Capital Expenditures. Only manufacturing companies that have substantial investments in capital expenditures are included in the sample. In the population for the 10-year period, about 70% of the 2478 companies have mean capital expenditures greater than $1 million per year. The mean amount of $1 million annually is used as the criterion. For the selected companies, mean capital expenditures for the 1980-1989 period is greater than $1 million per year.

Availability of Complete 10-Year Data. After first two criteria are satisfied, only companies with complete 10-year data are included in the sample. In the COMPUSTAT II files several foreign corporations began U.S. operations after the mid 1980s. For example, Toyota Motor Corporation was formed in the United States in 1982 and started its businesses in 1983. These foreign companies are not included even though they satisfy the earlier selection criteria. In the sample each selected company has complete 10-year data for each variable.

No Change in Inventory Valuation Methods. This study uses the APC productivity model, which is gross-profit oriented, to measure changes in productivity. Changes in inventory valuation methods may have an impact on gross profit and income figures, which are related to the two performance measures (i.e., productivity and profitability) used in this study. To remove this possibility, only companies reflecting no change in their inventory valuation methods during the 1980-1989 period are included in the sample. Changes in inventory valuation methods are indicated by changes in code numbers in COMPUSTAT.

After satisfying all the industry and company selection criteria, the research sample comprises 77 manufacturing companies in 20 industries. Appendix 1 lists the 20 industries and Appendix 2 lists the 77 companies.

Time Lag Consideration

The literature suggests that productivity may be improved by increased catalyst financial commitments and that profitability may be increased by productivity improvements as well as by increased catalyst financial commitments. However, the relationship between inputs and outputs may be negative or null in the current period and positive only after longer periods. The investment payback periods in the new manufacturing environment are shorter than three years (Howell and Soucy, 1988). Therefore, the study is confined to examinations of the relationships between increases in catalyst investments and changes in productivity and profitability in the year of the investment and succeeding two years. The SAS LAG function is used to examine lags between changes in substantial investments and the specified performance changes in the selected sample. Time lags for three variables (i.e., C_RD, C_CAP, and PRODUCT) for the Control Data Corporation are shown in Table 3.

STATISTICAL METHODOLOGY

Selection of statistical methods depends on the research purpose. This study investigates in the direction and strength of the relationships between variables. Correlation analysis, which measures the direction and the strength of the relationship between two variables, is therefore appropriate for the research. This measurement takes a numerical form called the correlation coefficient. SAS is used to compute correlation coefficients between variables. In addition to computing Pearson correlation coefficients, the SAS routines also provide the p-value, a measure of the strength of the evidence against the null hypothesis that there is no relationship between two variables. The smaller the p-value, the more likely a researcher would reject the null hypothesis. In this study, null hypotheses are tested at two significance levels (i.e., α =0.05,0.10). In Chapter Five, each table that presents results of testing hypotheses includes three columns: significant positive correlation, significant negative correlation, and nonsignificant correlation.

As shown in Table 5 immediately below, the relationship between changes in capital expenditures and changes in profitability for the Control Data Corporation is significantly positive at the 0.05 level in the year of the investment increase (see "No Lag" column, bottom). Changes in research and development expenses have significantly negative effects on productivity in the succeeding two years of investments (see both "One-Year Lag" and "Two-Year Lag" columns, top). For those same two years, changes in capital expenditures have significantly positive effects on productivity. The remaining correlations shown in Table 5 are not significant.

SUMMARY OF RESEARCH METHODOLOGY

The primary objective of this study is to examine empirically the five major relationships among four variables in the selected sample. Specific attention is focused on identifying the effects of increased investments in research and development and capital expenditures on two performance measures (i.e., productivity and profitability). Five null hypotheses are tested at the industry level and at the company level for up to two-year lags.

The scope of this research is limited to manufacturing companies with substantial investments in research and development projects and capital improvements. The COMPUSTAT II files serve as the database. The time frame for this study is the ten-year period 1980-1989. From the population of COMPUSTAT II, 77 companies in 20 industries satisfying all industry and company selection criteria are selected in the study.

Table 5
Correlation Table
Control Data Corporation

	No Lag	One-Year Lag	Two-Year Lag
Productivity and	-0.479	-0.899	-0.913
C_RD	0.192	0.002**	0.004**
Productivity and	0.570	0.732	0.708
C_CAP	0.109	0.039**	0.075*
Productivity and	0.526	0.290	0.084
C_ROA	0.146	0.487	0.858
C_ROA and	-0.073	-0.566	-0.442
C_RD	0.853	0.144	0.321
C_ROA and	0.732	-0.092	0.147
C_CAP	0.025**	0.829	0.752

Notes: The first number indicates the Pearson correlation coefficient.
The second number indicates the observed significance level
(or P-Value). Two asterisks(**) indicates significance at the
0.05 level. One asterisk(*) indicates significance only at the
0.10 level.

Because the research purpose is to measure the direction and
strength of the relationships between each pair of four variables,
correlation analysis is used for statistical analysis. The findings of this
study are expected to provide management accountants and researchers with information on the effects of substantial investments in

research and development and capital expenditures on changes in performance measures in selected industries and in certain companies within those industries.

V

Analyses of Key Relationships

This chapter presents findings on the relationships between changes in catalyst financial commitments (i.e., research and development projects and capital improvements) and changes in productivity and profitability, and the relationship between productivity and profitability. The sample of 77 companies in 20 industries was selected from the COMPUSTAT II files after satisfying both industry and company selection criteria. As stated earlier, the primary objective of this research is to investigate empirically the relationships among four variables (i.e., C_RD, C_CAP, Productivity, and C_ROA) in the selected industries and in certain companies within these industries over the 1980-1989 period. Since benefits of some investment projects are not realized in the year of the increase in investments, the study also considers time lags (i.e., one-year and two-year lags) between changes in substantial investments in research and development projects and capital improvements and changes in productivity and profitability.

MAJOR RELATIONSHIPS IN SELECTED INDUSTRIES

Figure 1 (Chapter One) depicts the five relationships among the four variables as the Study Focus Model. In seeking to determine the impacts of increased investments on changes in productivity and profitability, this study specifically is to answer the following research questions: (1) What are the impacts of changes in catalyst financial commitments on productivity changes? (2) Are there significant relationships between productivity changes and profitability changes? (3) What are the impacts of changes in catalyst financial commitments on profitability changes? (4) Do time lags exist between changes in substantial investments and productivity/profitability changes for the first and second year after the year of investment? Based on these questions, five hypotheses first are tested at the industry level. Due to the possibility of differences in benefits realization periods, the five relationships are tested in the year of the increase in investments and for each of the two succeeding years, respectively.

No Lag

Table 6 shows the results at two significance levels (i.e., $\alpha = 0.05$ and $\alpha = 0.10$). Since this study examines on the impact of increased investments on changes in productivity and profitability in the year of the increase in investments, Table 7 lists industries with significant correlations at two significance levels. The results are discussed below.

Research and Development Expenses and Productivity

As shown in Table 6, the first hypothesis — changes in research and development expenses are not related to productivity changes — is rejected in 7 of the 20 industries at the 0.05 significance level and in 10 of those industries at the 0.10 significance level. Seven industries with positive correlations are significant at the 0.05 level. Eight industries with positive correlations and two industries with negative correlations are significant at the 0.10 level. As shown in Table 7, the seven industries with positive correlations significant at the 0.05 level are food and kindred products, paper and allied products, paper mills, plastic materials, soap and detergent, semiconductor, and motor vehicles. The paperboard industry has a significant positive correlation only at the 0.10 level. The two industries (i.e., plastics and resins, and electronic computer) with negative correlations are significant only at the 0.10 level.

Capital Expenditures and Productivity

The second hypothesis — changes in investments in capital expenditures are not related to productivity changes — is rejected in 6 industries at the 0.05 significance level and in 7 industries at the 0.10 significance level. Table 6 shows that all of these correlations are positive. Industries with significant correlations as listed in Table 7 include paper and applied products, paper mills, chemicals and allied products, miscellaneous chemical products, computer and office equipment, semiconductor, and motor vehicles industries. The paper mills industry is significant only at the 0.10 level.

Table 6
No Lag: Five Major Relationships for 20 Industries

	Significant Positive Correlation		Significant Negative Correlation		Nonsignificant	
	5%	10%	5%	10%	5%	10%
Productivity and C_RD	7	8[*]	0	2	13	10
Productivity and C_CAP	6	7	0	0	14	13
C_ROA and Productivity	8	9	1	2	11	9
C_ROA and C_RD	3	3	0	0	17	17
C_ROA and C_CAP	4	6	1	2	15	12

Note: The number in each cell indicates the total number of industries in each category. Thus, the 8 industries with significance at the 0.10 level include the 7 industries with significance at the 0.05 level.

Table 7

No Lag: List of 20 Industries with Significant Correlations

SIC Code	Industry Name	(1)	(2)	(3)	(4)	(5)
2000	FOOD AND KINDRED PRODUCTS	+		+		
2040	GRAIN MILL PRODUCTS					+
2600	PAPER AND ALLIED PRODUCTS	+	+	+		
2621	PAPER MILLS	+	+*	+	+	
2670	ONVRT PAPR,PAPRBRD,EX BOXES	+*		+		
2800	CHEMICALS & ALLIED PRODS		+	+		
2820	PLASTIC MATL,SYNTHETIC RESIN	+		+	+	+*
2821	PLASTICS,RESINS,ELASTOMERS	-*				
2834	PHARMACEUTICAL PREPARATIONS			+	+	
2840	SOAP,DETERGENT,TOILET PREPS	+				-*
2851	PAINTS, VARNISHES, LACQUERS					+
2890	MISC CHEMICAL PRODUCTS		+			
3570	COMPUTER & OFFICE EQUIPMENT		+			+
3571	ELECTRONIC COMPUTERS	-*				
3621	MOTORS AND GENERATORS			+		+*
3663	RADIO,TV BROADCAST, COMM EQ			+		
3670	ELECTRONIC COMP, ACCESSORIES					
3674	SEMICONDUCTOR,RELATED DEVICE		+	+	+*	+
3711	MOTOR VEHICLES & CAR BODIES	+	+	-*		
3714	MOTOR VEHICLE PART,ACCESSORY			-		

Notes: One asterisk (*) indicates significance only at $\alpha = 0.10$.

(1): Productivity and C_RD; (2): Productivity and C_CAP;

(3) : C_ROA and Productivity;

(4): C_ROA and C_RD; (5) : C_ROA and C_CAP

+ : Significant positive correlation;

- : Significant negative correlation.

Productivity and Profitability

Table 6 shows the results for the third hypothesis that productivity changes have no effect on profitability changes. This hypothesis is rejected in 9 industries (i.e., 8 positive and 1 negative) at the 0.05 level and in 11 industries (i.e., 9 positive and 2 negative) at 0.10 level. Those industries with significant positive correlations at 0.05 level, as presented in Table 7, are the food and kindred products industries, three paper industries, two chemicals industries, and two electronics industries. The semiconductor industry has a significant positive correlation only at α =0.10. Both industries that show significant negative correlations for the third hypothesis are motor industries: the motor vehicle parts industry at α =0.05 and the motor vehicles industry at a = 0.10.

Research and Development Expenses and Profitability

As presented in Table 6, the fourth hypothesis—changes in research and development expenses are not related to profitability changes — is rejected in 3 of the 20 industries at two significance levels. These three industries with significant positive correlations as listed in Table 7 include paper mills, plastic material, and pharmaceutical preparations.

Capital Expenditures and Profitability

The fifth hypothesis—changes in investments in capital expenditures are not related to profitability changes—is rejected in 5 industries (i.e., 4 positive and 1 negative) at the 0.05 level, and in 8 industries (i.e., 6 positive and 2 negative) at the 0.10 level. These results are shown in Table 6. As listed in Table 7, four industries (i.e., pharmaceutical preparations, paints, computer, and semiconductor) have significant positive correlations at α =0.05, while the plastic material and motors and generators industries have significant positive correlations only at α =0.10. Two industries have significant negative correlations, the grain mill products industry at the 0.05 level, and the soap and detergent industry at the 0.10 level.

Observations on No Lag Relationships

Four positive relationships exist in three industries — paper mills, semiconductor, and plastic materials — in the year of the investment increase (i.e., no lag). Productivity is changed positively by increases in catalyst financial commitments, while profitability is changed positively by increases in productivity and investments in research and development in the paper mills industry. The semiconductor industry has the same three relationships as the paper mills industry, but increases in investments in capital expenditures have positive effects on profitability in the semiconductor industry. Increases in research and development projects improve productivity, and increases in productivity and catalyst investments improve profitability in the plastic materials industry.

One-Year Lag

The same five hypotheses are tested to examine whether productivity and profitability are changed by the previous year's investments in research and development projects and capital improvements. Table 8 presents the results, and Table 9 indicates which industries have significant correlations at the 0.05 and the 0.10 significance levels.

Research and Development Expenses and Productivity

The first hypothesis—changes in research and development expenses are not related to changes in productivity—is rejected in 6 (i.e., 5 positive and 1 negative) of the 20 industries at the 0.05 level and in 9 (i.e., 6 positive and 3 negative) of the industries at the 0.10 level. These results are shown in Table 8. As listed in Table 9, five industries (i.e., paper and allied products, paper mills, plastic material, soap and detergent, and semiconductor) with positive correlations and the electronic computers industry with a negative correlation are significant at 0.05 level. However, the paperboard industry with a positive correlation and two industries (i.e., pharmaceutical preparations and motor vehicle parts) with negative correlations are significant only at the 0.10 level.

Table 8
One-Year Lag: Five Major Relationships for 20 Industries

	Significant Positive Correlation		Significant Negative Correlation		Nonsignificant	
	5%	10%	5%	10%	5%	10%
Productivity and C_RD	5	6*	1	3	14	11
Productivity and C_CAP	2	4	1	3	17	13
C_ROA and Productivity	6	6	1	1	13	13
C_ROA and C_RD	3	3	2	3	15	14
C_ROA and C_CAP	2	2	1	1	17	17

Note: The number in each cell indicates the total number of industries in each category. Thus, the 6 industries with significance at the 0.10 level include the 5 industries with significance at the 0.05 level.

Table 9

No Lag: List of 20 Industries with Significant Correlations Relationship

SIC Code	Industry Name	(1)	(2)	(3)	(4)	(5)
2000	FOOD AND KINDRED PRODUCTS			+		
2040	GRAIN MILL PRODUCTS					-*
2600	PAPER AND ALLIED PRODUCTS	+		+		
2621	PAPER MILLS	+		+	+	
2670	ONVRT PAPR,PAPRBRD,EX BOXES	+*				
2800	CHEMICALS & ALLIED PRODS		+*	+		
2820	PLASTIC MATL,SYNTHETIC RESIN	+		+	+	
2821	PLASTICS,RESINS,ELASTOMERS			-		
2834	PHARMACEUTICAL PREPARATIONS	-*			+	+
2840	SOAP,DETERGENT,TOILET PREPS	+				
2851	PAINTS, VARNISHES, LACQUERS					
2890	MISC CHEMICAL PRODUCTS		+			
3570	COMPUTER & OFFICE EQUIPMENT		+			
3571	ELECTRONIC COMPUTERS	-	-*			
3621	MOTORS AND GENERATORS			+		
3663	RADIO,TV BROADCAST, COMM EQ			-		
3670	ELECTRONIC CQMP, ACCESSORIES			-		-
3674	SEMICONDUCTOR,RELATED DEVICE	+	+*			
3711	MOTOR VEHICLES & CAR BODIES					+
3714	MOTOR VEHICLE PART,ACCESSORY	-*	-*	-		

Notes: One asterisk (*) indicates significance only at $\alpha = 0.10$.

       (1): Productivity and C_RD; (2): Productivity and C_CAP;

       (3) : C_ROA and Productivity; (4): C_ROA and C_RD;

       (5) : C_ROA and C_CAP

        + : Significant positive correlation;

        - : Significant negative correlation.

Capital Expenditures and Productivity

As presented in Table 8, the second hypothesis — changes in investments in capital expenditures are not related to productivity changes — is reflected in 3 industries (i.e., 2 positive and 1 negative) at the 0.05 level and in 7 industries (i.e., 4 positive and 3 negative) at the 0.10 level. Table 9 lists industries with significant correlations at two significance levels. Two industries (i.e. miscellaneous chemicals and computer and office equipment) with positive correlations and the plastics and resins industry with a negative correlation are significant at $\alpha = 0.05$. In addition, two industries (i.e., chemicals and allied products and semiconductor) with positive correlations and two other industries (i.e., electronic computers and motor vehicle parts) with negative correlations are significant only at $\alpha = 0.10$.

Productivity and Profitability

The third hypothesis — productivity changes have no effect on profitability changes — is rejected in 7 (i.e., 6 positive and 1 negative) of the 20 industries at the two significance levels as shown in Table 8. Industries with significant correlations are listed in Table 9. The positive relationship between productivity and profitability exists in six industries, including food and kindred products, paper and allied products, paper mills, chemicals and allied products, plastic materials, and motors and generators. A negative relationship between productivity and profitability exists in the motor vehicle parts industry.

Research and Development Expenses and Profitability

As shown in Table 8, the fourth hypothesis—changes in investments in research and development projects are not related to profitability changes—is rejected in 5 industries (i.e., 3 positive and 2 negative) at the 0.05 level and in 6 industries (i.e., 3 positive and 3 negative) at the 0.10 level. Three industries (i.e., paper mills, plastic material, and pharmaceutical preparations) have significant positive correlations at two significance levels as listed in Table 9. Three other industries have significant negative correlations: the radio and TV and electronic components industries at the 0.05 level, and the grain mill products industry at the 0.10 level.

Capital Expenditures and Profitability

The fifth hypothesis—changes in investments in capital expenditures are not related to profitability changes—is rejected in 3 industries (i.e., 2 positive and 1 negative) at two significance levels as shown in Table 8. As listed in Table 9, two industries (i.e., pharmaceutical preparations and motor vehicles and car bodies) have significant positive correlations. The electronic component industry has a negative correlation. In this industry the effect of changes in capital expenditures on profitability is negative.

Observations on One-Year Lag Relationships

Two industries (i.e., paper mills and plastic materials) have three positive relationships at the one-year lag point; the motor vehicle parts industry has three negative relationships one year after the increase in investments. Productivity is changed positively by increases in investments in research and development, and profitability is changed by increases in productivity and investments in research and development in the paper mills industry and the plastic materials industry. However, the relationships between changes in catalyst financial commitments and productivity changes and the relationship between productivity changes and profitability changes are negative in the motor vehicle parts industry. In addition, changes in research and development expenses have negative effects on productivity, but changes in investments in catalyst financial commitments have positive effects on profitability in the pharmaceutical industry.

Two-Year Lag

The results of the tests of the five hypotheses for the same relationships two years after the year of the pertinent expenditures are shown in Table 10. Industries with significant correlations are listed in Table 11.

Table 10
Two-Year Lag: Five Major Relationships for 20 Industries

	Significant Positive Correlation		Significant Negative Correlation		Nonsignificant	
	5%	10%	5%	10%	5%	10%
Productivity and C_RD	3	4[*]	2	3	15	13
Productivity and C_CAP	3	4	1	2	16	14
C_ROA and Productivity	6	7	0	0	14	13
C_ROA and C_RD	3	4	1	2	16	14
C_ROA and C_CAP	2	3	2	4	16	13

Note: The number in each cell indicates the total number of industries in each category. Thus, the 4 industries with significance at the 0.10 level include the 3 industries with significance at the 0.05 level.

Table 11

Two-Year Lag: List of 20 Industries with Significant Correlations

SIC Code	Industry Name	Relationship				
		(1)	(2)	(3)	(4)	(5)
2000	FOOD AND KINDRED PRODUCTS			+		-*
2040	GRAIN MILL PRODUCTS			-		
2600	PAPER AND ALLIED PRODUCTS	+*	+*	+		+*
2621	PAPER MILLS	+		+	+	-
2670	CONVRT PAPR,PAPRBRD,EX BOXES			+*		
2800	CHEMICALS & ALLIED PRODS					-*
2820	PLASTIC MATL,SYNTHETIC RESIN	+		+	+	
2821	PLASTICS,RESINS,ELASTOMERS		-			
2834	PHARMACEUTICAL PREPARATIONS	-*			+	+
2840	SOAP,DETERGENT,TOILET PREPS	+				
2851	PAINTS, VARNISHES, LACQUERS					
2890	MISC CHEMICAL PRODUCTS		+			
3570	COMPUTER & OFFICE EQUIPMENT		+			
3571	ELECTRONIC COMPUTERS	-	-*			
3621	MOTORS AND GENERATORS			+		
3663	RADIO,TV BROADCAST, COMM EQ					
3670	ELECTRONIC CQMP, ACCESSORIES				-*	-
3674	SEMICONDUCTOR,RELATED DEVICE					
3711	MOTOR VEHICLES & CAR BODIES		+	+	+*	
3714	MOTOR VEHICLE PART,ACCESSORY	-				+

Notes: One asterisk (*) indicates significance only at $\alpha = 0.10$.

(1): Productivity and C_RD; (2): Productivity and C_CAP;

(3) : C_ROA and Productivity; (4): C_ROA and C_RD;

(5) : C_ROA and C_CAP.

+ : Significant positive correlation;

- : Significant negative correlation.

Research and Development Expenses and Productivity

As shown in Table 10, the first hypothesis-changes in investments in research and development are not related changes in productivity-is rejected in 5 (i.e., 3 positive and 2 negative) of the 20 industries at the 0.05 level and in 7 (i.e., 4 positive and 3 negative) of those industries at the 0.10 level. Table 11 lists the industries with significant correlations. Three industries (i.e., paper mills, plastic materials, and soap and detergent) have positive relationships and two other industries (i.e., electronic computers and motor vehicle parts) have negative relationships at the 0.05 level. The paper and allied products industry with a positive correlation and the pharmaceutical preparations industry with a negative correlation are significant only at the 0.10 level.

Capital Expenditures and Productivity

The second hypothesis — changes in investments in capital expenditures are not related to changes in productivity — is rejected in 4 industries (i.e., 3 positive and 1 negative) at the 0.05 level and in 6 industries (i.e., 4 positive and 2 negative) at the 0.10 level as presented in Table 10. As listed in Table 11, three industries (i.e., miscellaneous chemical products, computer and office equipment, and motor vehicles) with positive correlations and the plastics and resins industry with a negative correlation are significant at α =0.05. The paper and allied products industry has a significant positive correlation and the electronic computers industry has a significant negative correlation only at α =0.10.

Productivity and Profitability

As shown in Table 10, the third hypothesis — productivity changes have no impact on profitability changes — is rejected in 6 industries at the 0.05 level and in 7 industries at the 0.10 level. All of the correlations are positive. As shown in Table 11, six industries (i.e., food and kindred products, paper and allied products, paper mills, plastic materials, motors and generators, and motor vehicles) are significant at the 0.05 level, while the paperboard industry is significant only at the 0.10 level.

Research and Development Expenses and Profitability

The fourth hypothesis — changes in investments in research and development are not related to changes in profitability — is rejected in 4 industries (i.e., 3 positive and 1 negative) at the 0.05 level and in 6 industries (i.e., 4 positive and 2 negative) at the 0.10 level as presented in Table 10. As listed in Table 11, three industries (i.e., paper mills, plastic materials, and pharmaceutical preparations) with positive correlations and the grain mill products industry with a negative correlation are significant at the 0.05 level. However, the motor vehicles industry with a positive correlation and the electronic component industry with a negative correlation are significant only at the 0.10 level.

Capital Expenditures and Profitability

The fifth hypothesis — changes in investments in capital expenditures are not related to changes in profitability — is rejected in 4 industries (i.e., 2 positive and 2 negative) at the 0.05 level and in 7 industries (i.e., 3 positive and 4 negative) at the 0.10 level. These results are shown in Table 10. Industries with significant correlations are listed in Table 11. Two industries (i.e., pharmaceutical preparations and motor vehicle parts) with positive correlations and two other industries i.e., paper mills and electronic component) with negative correlations are significant at a = 0.05. The paper and allied products industry with a positive correlation and two industries (i.e., food and kindred products and chemicals and allied products) with negative correlations are significant only at α =0.10.

Observations on Two-Year Lag Relationships

Benefits of investment projects are not realized until two years after investments in two paper industries. Increases in catalyst financial commitments change productivity, and increases in productivity as well as capital expenditures change profitability in the paper and allied products industry. Four other positive relationships exist in the paper mills industry. Productivity is changed by increases in investments in research and development projects and profitability is changed by increases in productivity and catalyst investments.

Summary Observations on Industry Relationships

The findings identify significant positive or negative relationships among the variables. Positive relationships imply that increased investments in research and development projects and/or capital improvements have positive effects on productivity and/or profitability. The results of the tests of the five hypothesized relationships at the industry level show that one or more positive relationships exist in each of 16 industries. Some of these industries will be further discussed below. Four industries — grain mill products, plastics and resins, electronic computer, and electronic components—have one or more negative relationships in the study period. Negative relationships imply that a company has not made wise investments. Because each of these four industries is represented by very few companies in the sample (see Appendix 1), making reasonable conjectures about the reasons for these results is very difficult.

For the industries with positive relationships, some investment projects affect productivity and/or profitability in the year of investment. For example, changes in research and development have positive effects on productivity in the food and kindred products industry, and changes in capital expenditures have positive effects on profitability in the computer and office equipment industry in the investment year. One can speculate that research projects to create new or improved products in the food and kindred products industry helps increase demand and thus output. Once output is increased, productivity increases. In the computer and office equipment industry, companies that invest wisely in automation evidentially improve their operating efficiency and thus their profitability.

In other industries, the benefits of investments are realized in future periods. In the motor vehicles industry, for example, changes in capital expenditures have positive effects on profitability in the one-year lag period, and changes in research and development have positive effects on profitability in the two-year lag period. The literature suggests that automobile companies usually make substantial investments in research and development projects before their investments in capital expenditures. Once models for new cars are created, these companies purchase necessary equipment for efficient production in order to achieve additional advantages in the competitive market. The one-year lag and two-year lag results for this industry thus may reflect this design/production pattern.

This study is particularly interested in industries with the same relationships for all three periods, because investments in these types of industries seem to be more effective. As shown in Table 12, there are ten industries with one or more significant relationships for all three periods (i.e., no lag, one-year lag, and two-year lag). One relationship exists in each of six industries: soap and detergent, electronic computer, miscellaneous chemicals, computer and office equipment, food and kindred products, and motors and generators. Two industries — paper and allied products and pharmaceutical preparations — have two significant positive relationships for all three periods. In addition, three relationships are significantly positive at the 0.05 level in the paper mills industry and the plastic materials industry.

In several instances, two industries show the same relationships for all three periods in the findings. The second relationship — changes in capital expenditures are related to changes in productivity — exists in both the miscellaneous chemicals and the computer and office equipment industries. The third relationship changes in productivity are related to changes in profitability — exists in two other industries: food and kindred products, and motors and generators. In addition, three identical relationships exist in both the paper mills and the plastic material industries. Changes in research and development expenses have positive effects on both productivity and profitability, and changes in productivity also have a positive impact on changes in profitability in these two industries.

Furthermore, the first relationship — changes in research and development expenses are related to changes in productivity — exists in two industries: soap and detergent and electronic computer. In this case, the relationship is significantly positive (at the 0.05 level) in the soap and detergent industry, but significantly negative (at the 0.10 level) in the electronic computer industry. Since the electronic computer industry is a high technology industry, the effects of ineffective investments can conceivably cause major declines in output that lead to decreases in productivity for several years.

MAJOR RELATIONSHIPS IN SELECTED COMPANIES

Based on the four research questions in this study, the five hypotheses are tested at the company level. Benefits of investment projects can be realized in the year of the increase in investments, or in the future years. The five relationships are tested in the year when investments are increased and for each of the two succeeding years, respectively.

Table 12
Significant Relationships for Three Periods
in Selected Industries

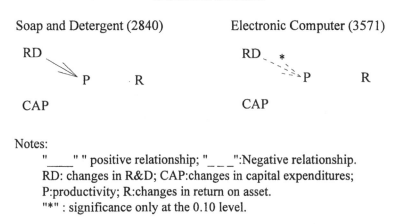

Soap and Detergent (2840)   Electronic Computer (3571)

Notes:
"____" " positive relationship; "_ _ _":Negative relationship.
RD: changes in R&D; CAP:changes in capital expenditures;
P:productivity; R:changes in return on asset.
"*" : significance only at the 0.10 level.

Table 12 (Continued)
Significant Relationships for Three Periods
in Selected Industries

Mise Chemicals (2890)   Computer and Office Equipment (3570)

RD   RD

      P   R   P   R

CAP   CAP

Food and Kindred (2000)   Motors and Generators (3621)

RD   RD

    P ⟶ R   P ⟶ R

CAP   CAP

Paper and Allied (2600)   Pharmaceutical (2834)

RD   *   RD

     P ⟶ R   P ⟶ R

CAP   CAP

Paper Mills (2621)   Plastic Matl (2820)

RD   RD

     P ⟶ R   P ⟶ R

CAP   CAP

Notes:
"_____" " positive relationship; "_ _ _ _":Negative relationship.
RD: changes in R&D; CAP:changes in capital expenditures;
P:productivity; R:changes in return on asset.
"*" : significance only at the 0.10 level.

No Lag

The results for the five relationships at two significance levels (i.e., α =0.05 and α =0.10) are shown in Table 13. All 77 companies in the sample are listed in Table 14. Positive and negative correlations for each of the five relationships in the investment year (no lag) are indicated by plus or minus signs, respectively.

As noted in Table 14, "Pre FASB" indicates data that do not reflect implementation of the Statement of Financial Accounting Standard No. 94, Consolidation of All Majority-Owned Subsidiaries, effective for fiscal years beginning on or after December 16,1988. In the sample, three companies-Ethyl Ford, and General Motors—have two kinds of financial reports (i.e., with implementation and without implementation of FASB-94). If these three companies with "Pre FASB" are eliminated from the sample, findings for the industry level are almost the same, except for one relationship. The third relationship—changes in productivity are related to changes in profitability—was significantly negative in the motor vehicles industry (see Table 7). This relationship becomes nonsignificant in that industry when the "Pre FASB" data for Ford and General Motors are deleted.

Research and Development Expenses and Productivity

As shown in Table 13, the first hypothesis—changes in research and development expenses are not related to changes in productivity — is rejected in 37 (i.e., 33 positive and 4 negative) of the 77 companies at the 0.05 significance level and in 42 (i.e., 38 positive and 4 negative) of those companies at the 0.10 significance level. As Table 14 reflects, 33 companies (i.e., 6 food, 5 paper, 18 chemicals, 1 computer, 1 electronics, and 2 motor) with positive correlations and 4 companies (i.e., 2 chemicals, 1 computer, and 1 motor) with negative correlations are significant at the 0.05 level. Five companies (i.e., 1 paper, 2 chemicals, and 2 motor) with positive correlations are significant only at the 0.10 level.

Table 13

No Lag: Five Major Relationships for 77 Industries

	Significant Positive Correlation		Significant Negative Correlation		Nonsignificant	
	5%	10%	5%	10%	5%	10%
Productivity and C_RD	33	38[*]	4	4	40	35
Productivity and C_CAP	20	28	5	6	52	43
C_ROA and Productivity	26	33	6	7	45	37
C_ROA and C_RD	12	13	5	9	60	55
C_ROA and C_CAP	10	15	4	5	63	57

Note: The number in each cell indicates the total number of industries in each category. Thus, the 6 industries with significance at the 0.10 level include the 5 industries with significance at the 0.05 level.

Table 14

No Lag: List of 77 Companies with Significant Correlations

SIC Code	Industry Name	Relationship				
		(1)	(2)	(3)	(4)	(5)
2000	BORDEN INC	+	+			
2000	CAMPBELL SOUP CO	+	+			
2000	UNILEVER PLC-AMER SHRS	+	+*	+	+	+
2000	UNILEVER N V-NY SHARES	+	+	+	+	+
2040	KELLOGG CO	+	+	-	-*	-
2040	RALSTON PURINA CO	+				
2600	INTL PAPER CO	+	+*			
2600	MEAD CORP			+		
2621	BOISE CASCADE CORP	+	+*	+	+	
2621	DOMTAR INC	+	+			
2621	KIMBERLY-CLARK CORP	+				
2621	UNION CAMP CORP			+*		
2621	WESTVACO CORP	+	+	+*		
2670	BEMIS CO	+*	+*	+	+	+
2670	DENNISON MFG CO					
2670	NASHUA CORP					
2800	AMERICAN CYANAMID CO	+	+			
2800	ETHYL CORP	+				
2800	ETHYL CORP-PRE FASB	+		+	+	+*
2800	FMC CORP	+				
2800	FERRO CORP	+	+*	+	+	+

Notes: One asterisk (*) indicates significance only at $\alpha = 0.10$.
      (1): Productivity and C_RD; (2): Productivity and C_CAP;
      (3) : C_ROA and Productivity; (4): C_ROA and C_RD;
      (5) : C_ROA and C_CAP.
      + : Significant positive correlation;
      - : Significant negative correlation.
      Pre FASB: Without Implementation of FASB_94, Consolidation of
      ALL Majority-Owned Subsidiaries.

Table 14 (Continued)
No Lag: List of 77 Industries with Significant Correlations

SIC Code	Industry Name	Relationship				
		(1)	(2)	(3)	(4)	(5)
2800	HERCULES INC	+*	+			
2800	IMPERIAL CHEN INDS PLC-ADR	+	+	+	+	+
2800	OLIN CORP					
2820	DU PONT (E.I.) DE NEMOURS	+		+	+	+*
2821	DEXTER CORP				-*	
2821	GOODRICH (B.F.) CO					
2821	UNION CARBIDE CORP		-			
2834	ABBOTT LABORATORIES	+	+	+	+	+
2834	BAXTER INTERNATIONAL INC	-	-			
2834	BRISTOL MYERS SQUIBB	+	+			-
2834	CARTER-WALLACE INC	+		+	+	+
2834	FOREST LABORATORIES-CL A	-	-			
2834	JOHNSON & JOHNSON	+	+			
2834	LILLY (ELI) & CO	+	+			
2834	MARION MERRELL DOW INC	+	+	+	+	+
2834	MYLAN LABORATORIES		+	+		
2834	WARNER-LAMBERT CO	+				
2840	CHEMED CORP		-			
2840	COLGATE-PALMOLIVE CO	+*				-
2840	PROCTER & GAMBLE CO	+		-*	-	-
2851	DE SOTO INC					
2851	PPG INDUSTRIES INC	+		+	+*	

Notes: One asterisk (*) indicates significance only at α =0.10.
     (1): Productivity and C_RD; (2): Productivity and C_CAP;
     (3) : C_ROA and Productivity; (4): C_ROA and C_RD;
     (5) : C_ROA and C_CAP.
     + : Significant positive correlation;
     - : Significant negative correlation.
     Pre FASB: Without Implementation of FASB_94, Consolidation of
     ALL Majority-Owned Subsidiaries.*

Table 14 (Continued)
No Lag: List of 77 Industries with Significant Correlations

SIC Code	Industry Name	(1)	(2)	(3)	(4)	(5)
2851	PRATT & LAMBERT INC			+		
2851	SHERWIN-WILLIAMS CO	+	+*	+	+	
2890	BETZ LABORATORIES INC	+	+*	-	-*	
2890	LAWTER INTERNATIONAL INC		+			
2890	NALCO CHEMICAL CO		+			
3570	CONTROL DATA CORP					+
3570	DATA GENERAL CORP				-	
3570	DIGITAL EQUIPMENT	+	+	+		+*
3570	HEWLETT-PACKARD CO					
3570	INTL BUSINESS MACHINES CORP	-		+	-	
3570	WANG LABORATORIES-CL B		-*		-	
3571	COMMODORE INTL LTD			+		
3571	FLOATING POINT SYSTEMS INC			+		+*
3621	BALDOR ELECTRIC			+*		
3621	EMERSON ELECTRIC CO			-		
3621	KOLLMLRGEN CORP			+*		+
3621	VERNITRON CORP					
3663	ANDREW CORP			+		
3663	AYDIN CORP				-*	
3663	GENERAL INSTRUMENT CORP			+		
3663	SCIENTIFIC-ATLANTA INC			+		
3670	CTS CORP					

Notes: One asterisk (*) indicates significance only at $\alpha = 0.10$.
    (1): Productivity and C_RD; (2): Productivity and C_CAP;
    (3) : C_ROA and Productivity; (4): C_ROA and C_RD;
    (5) : C_ROA and C_CAP.
    + : Significant positive correlation;
    - : Significant negative correlation.
    Pre FASB: Without Implementation of FASB_94, Consolidation of
    ALL Majority-Owned Subsidiaries.*

Table 14 (Continued)
No Lag: List of 77 Industries with Significant Correlations

		Relationship				
SIC Code	Industry Name	(1)	(2)	(3)	(4)	(5)
3670	VARTAN ASSOCIATES INC			+*		
3674	ADVANCED MICRO DEVICES	+	+			
3674	INTL RECTIFIER CORP			+*		
3674	UNITRODE CORP		+		+	+*
3711	FORD MOTOR CO	+	+			
3711	FORD MOTOR CO-PRE FASB	+	+*	-		
3711	GENERAL MOTOR CORP	+*				
3711	GENERAL MOTOR CORP-PRE FASB			-		
3714	ECHLIN INC	-	-	+*		-*
3714	SMITH (A.O) CORP-CL A		-			
3714	SPARTON CORP			+		
3714	STANDARD PRODUCTS CO	+*	+	-		

Notes: One asterisk (*) indicates significance only at $\alpha = 0.10$.
       (1): Productivity and C_RD; (2): Productivity and C_CAP;
       (3) : C_ROA and Productivity; (4): C_ROA and C_RD;
       (5) : C_ROA and C_CAP.
       + : Significant positive correlation;
       - : Significant negative correlation.
       Pre FASB: Without Implementation of FASB_94, Consolidation of
ALL Majority-Owned Subsidiaries.*

Capital Expenditures and Productivity

The second hypothesis — changes in capital expenditures are not related to changes in productivity — is rejected in 25 companies (i.e., 20 positive and 5 negative) at the 0.05 level and in 34 companies (i.e., 28 positive and 6 negative) at the 0.10 level, as shown in Table 13. As Table 14 indicates, 20 companies (i.e., 4 food, 2 paper, 9 chemicals, 1 computer, 2 electronics, and 2 motor) with positive correlations and 5 companies (i.e.,

4 chemicals and 1 motor) with negative correlations are significant at the 0.05 level. Eight companies (i.e., 1 food, 3 paper, 3 chemicals, and 1 motor) with positive correlations and one computer company with a negative correlation are significant only at the 0.10 level.

Productivity and Profitability

As presented in Table 13, the third hypothesis—productivity changes have no effect on profitability changes—is rejected in 32 companies (i.e., 26 positive and 6 negative) at the 0.05 level and in 40 companies (i.e., 33 positive and 7 negative) at the 0.10 level. As Table 14 reflects, 26 companies (i.e., 2 food, 3 paper, 12 chemicals, 4 computer, 4 electronics, and 1 motor) with positive correlations and 6 companies (i.e., 1 food, 2 chemicals, and 3 motor) with negative correlations are significant at $\alpha = 0.05$. Seven companies (i.e., 2 paper, 4 electronics, and 1 motor) with positive correlations and one chemicals company with a negative correlation are significant only at $\alpha = 0.10$.

Research and Development Expenses and Profitability

The fourth hypothesis — changes in research and development expenses are not related to profitability changes — is rejected in 17 companies i.e.,., 12 positive and 5 negative) at the 0.05 level and in 22 companies (i.e., 13 positive and 9 negative) at the 0.10 level as shown in Table 13. As Table 14 illustrates, 12 companies (i.e., 2 food, 2 paper, and 8 chemicals) with positive correlations and 5 companies (i.e., 1 chemicals, 3 computer, and 1 electronics) with negative correlations are significant at the 0.05 level. One chemicals company with a positive correlation and four companies (i.e., 1 food, 2 chemicals, and 1 electronics) with negative correlations are significant at the 0.10 level.

Capital Expenditures and Profitability

The fifth hypothesis—changes in capital expenditures are not related to profitability changes—is rejected in 14 companies (i.e., 10 positive and 4 negative) at the 0.05 level and in 20 companies i.e.,., 15 positive and 5 negative) at the 0.10 level as presented in Table 13. As Table 14 reflects, 10 companies (i.e., 2 food, 1 paper, 5 chemicals, 1 computer, and 1 electronics) with positive correlations and 4 companies (i.e., 1 food and 3 chemicals) with negative correlations are significant at α =0.05. Five companies (i.e., 2 chemicals, 2 computer, and 1 electronics) with positive correlations and one motor company with a negative correlation are significant only at α =0.10.

Observations on No Lag Relationships

Five positive relationships exist for seven companies—Unilever PLC, Unilever N V, Bemis, Ferro, Imperial Chernicals, Abbott Laboratories, and Marion Merrell Dow — in the year of increased investments. In addition, Kellogg Corporation has two positive relationships and three negative relationships. Kellogg's increases in catalyst financial commitments improve productivity, but increases in productivity and catalyst investments have negative effects on profitability.

One-Year Lag

The same five hypotheses are tested to investigate whether productivity and/or profitability is changed by the previous year's investments in research and development and capital improvements. Table 15 presents the results at the two significance levels. Table 16 indicates companies with significant correlations at α = 0.05 and α = 0.10.

Research and Development Expenses and Productivity

As shown in Table 15, the first hypothesis—changes in research and development expenses are not related to changes in productivity — is rejected in 39 (i.e., 31 positive and 8 negative) of the 77 companies at the 0.05 significance level and in 47 (i.e., 35 positive and 12 negative) of those companies at the 0.10 significance level. As Table 16 reflects, 31 companies (i.e., 5 food, 3 paper, 19 chemicals, 2 computer, and 2 motor) with positive correlations and 8 companies (i.e., 2 chemicals, 3 computer, 1 electronics, and 2 motor) with negative correlations are significant at the

0.05 level. Four companies (i.e., 1 food, 1 paper, 1 chemicals, and 1 motor) with positive correlations and four other companies (i.e., 1 computer and 3 electronics) with negative correlations are significant only at the 0.10 level.

Capital Expenditures and Productivity

The second hypothesis — changes in capital expenditures are not related to changes in productivity — is rejected in 27 companies (i.e., 19 positive and 8 negative) at the 0.05 level and in 29 companies (i.e., 20 positive and 9 negative) at the 0.10 level as shown in Table 15. As Table 16 indicates, 19 companies (i.e., 4 food, 2 paper, 9 chemicals, 2 computer, and 2 motor) with positive correlations and 8 companies (i.e., 4 chemicals, 1 computer, 2 electronics, and 1 motor) with negative correlations are significant at the 0.05 level. One computer company with a positive correlation and one motor company with a negative correlation are significant only at the 0.10 level.

Productivity and Profitability

As presented in Table 15, the third hypothesis productivity changes have no effect on profitability changes — is rejected in 19 companies (i.e., 17 positive and 2 negative) at the 0.05 level and in 28 companies (i.e., 22 positive and 6 negative) at the 0.10 level. As Table 16 reflects, 17 companies (i.e., 1 food, 5 paper, 8 chemicals, 2 computer, and 1 electronics) with positive correlations and 2 food companies with negative correlations are significant at $\alpha = 0.05$. Five companies (i.e., 1 food, 1 paper, 1 chemicals, 1 computer, and 1 electronics) with positive correlations and four companies (i.e., 2 chemicals, 1 electronics, and 1 motor) with negative correlations are significant only at $\alpha = 0.10$.

Table 15
No Lag: Five Major Relationships for 77 Industries

	Significant Positive Correlation		Significant Negative Correlation		Nonsignificant	
	5%	10%	5%	10%	5%	10%
Productivity and C_RD	31	35*	8	12	38	30
Productivity and C_CAP	19	20	8	9	50	49
C_ROA and Productivity	17	22	2	6	58	49
C_ROA and C_RD	11	14	12	20	54	43
C_ROA and C_CAP	5	7	6	8	66	62

Note: The number in each cell indicates the total number of industries in each category. Thus, the 35 companies with significance at the 0.10 level include the 31 companies with significance at the 0.05 level.

Table 16

One-Year Lag: List of 77 Companies with Significant Correlations

SIC Code	Company Name	Relationship				
		(1)	(2)	(3)	(4)	(5)
2000	BORDEN INC	+	+		-*	
2000	CAMPBELL SOUP CO	+	+	-	-*	-
2000	UNILEVER PLC-AMER SHRS	+		+	+	
2000	UNILEVER N V-NY SHARES	+*	+	+*	+	+
2040	KELLOGG CO	+	+	-	-	-
2040	RALSTON PURINA CO	+				
2600	INTL PAPER CO	+		+	+	
2600	MEAD CORP			+		
2621	BOISE CASCADE CORP	+*		+		
2621	DOMTAR INC		+		-*	
2621	KIMBERLY-CLARK CORP	+		+	+	
2621	UNION CAMP CORP					
2621	WESTVACO CORP	+	+	+*	+*	
2670	BEMIS CO			+		
2670	DENNISON MFG CO					
2670	NASHUA CORP			-		
2800	AMERICAN CYANAMID CO	+	+			
2800	ETHYL CORP	+				-*
2800	ETHYL CORP-PRE FASB	+		+	+	
2800	FMC CORP	+				
2800	FERRO CORP	+	+		+	

Notes: One asterisk (*) indicates significance only at $\alpha = 0.10$.

(1): Productivity and C_RD; (2): Productivity and C_CAP;

(3) : C_ROA and Productivity; (4): C_ROA and C RD;

(5) : C_ROA and C CAP.

+ : Significant positive correlation;

- : Significant negative correlation.

Pre FASB: Without Implementation of FASB-94, Consolidation of ALL Majority-Owned Subsidiaries.

Table 16 (Continued)

One-Year Lag: List of 77 Companies with Significant Correlations

SIC Code	Industry Name	Relationship				
		(1)	(2)	(3)	(4)	(5)
2800	HERCULES INC	+*				
2800	IMPERIAL CHEN INDS PLC-ADR	+	+	+*	+*	+*
2800	OLIN CORP					
2820	DU PONT (E.I.) DE NEMOURS	+		+	+	
2821	DEXTER CORP					
2821	GOODRICH (B.F.) CO					
2821	UNION CARBIDE CORP		-		-	
2834	ABBOTT LABORATORIES	+	+	+	+	+
2834	BAXTER INTERNATIONAL INC	-	-			
2834	BRISTOL MYERS SQUIBB	+	+			
2834	CARTER-WALLACE INC	+		+	+	+
2834	FOREST LABORATORIES-CL A	-	-			
2834	JOHNSON & JOHNSON	+	+			
2834	LILLY (ELI) & CO	+	+			
2834	MARION MERRELL DOW INC	+	+	+	+	+
2834	MYLAN LABORATORIES					
2834	WARNER-LAMBERT CO	+				
2840	CHEMED CORP		-			
2840	COLGATE-PALMOLIVE CO		+		-*	
2840	PROCTER & GAMBLE CO	+	+			-
2851	DE SOTO INC	+				
2851	PRG INDUSTRIES INC	+		+	+	

Notes: One asterisk (*) indicates significance only at α =0.10.

(1): Productivity and C_RD; (2): Productivity and C_CAP;

(3) : C_ROA and Productivity; (4): C_ROA and C_RD;

(5) : C_ROA and C_CAP.

+ : Significant positive correlation;

- : Significant negative correlation.

Pre FASB: Without Implementation of FASB-94, Consolidation of ALL Majority-Owned Subsidiaries.

Table 16 (Continued)
One-Year Lag: List of 77 Companies with Significant Correlations

			Relationship			
SIC Code	Industry Name	(1)	(2)	(3)	(4)	(5)
2851	PRATT & LAMBERT INC					
2851	SHERWIN-WILLIAMS INC	+		+	+*	
2890	BETZ LABORATORIES INC	+			-*	
2890	LAWTER INTERNATIONAL INC					
2890	NALCO CHEMICAL CO			-*		-
3570	CONTROL DATA CORP	-		+		
3570	DATA GENERAL CORP	+			-	
3570	DIGITAL EQUIPMENT	+	+			
3570	HEWLETT-PACKARD CO					-*
3570	INTL BUSINESS MACHINES CORP	-	+*	+	-	
3570	WANG LABORATORIES-CL B		-*		-	
3571	COMMODORE INTL LTD		-		-	
3571	FLOATING POINT SYSTEMS INC	-*		+	-*	
3621	BALDOR ELECTRIC					
3621	EMERSON ELECTRIC CO				-	
3621	KOLLMLRGEN CORP	-			-	
3621	VERNITRON CORP					
3663	ANDREW CORP				-*	
3663	AYDIN CORP			-*	-	
3663	GENERAL INSTRUMENT CORP			+*	-	
3663	SCIENTIFIC-ATLANTA INC		-			
3670	CTS CORP					

Notes: One asterisk (*) indicates significance only at α =0.10.
   (1): Productivity and C_RD; (2): Productivity and C_CAP;
   (3) : C_ROA and Productivity; (4): C_ROA and C_RD;
   (5) : C_ROA and C_CAP.
    + : Significant positive correlation;
    - : Significant negative correlation.
   Pre FASB: Without Implementation of FASB-94, Consolidation of
   ALL Majority-Owned Subsidiaries.

Table 16 (Continued)

One-Year Lag: List of 77 Companies with Significant Correlations

SIC Code	Industry Name	Relationship				
		(1)	(2)	(3)	(4)	(5)
3670	VARTAN ASSOCIATES INC	-*			-*	-
3674	ADVANCED MICRO DEVICES					
3674	INTL RECTIFIER CORP	-*	-			
3674	UNITRODE CORP	-*		+		
3711	FORD MOTOR CO	+	+			
3711	FORD MOTOR CO-PRE FASB	+*		-*		
3711	GENERAL MOTOR CORP					+*
3711	GENERAL MOTOR CORP-PRE FASB		-*			+
3714	ECHLIN INC	-	-		-	-
3714	SMITH (A.O) CORP-CL A					
3714	SPARTON CORP	-			-	
3714	STANDARD PRODUCTS CO	+	+			

Notes: One asterisk (*) indicates significance only at α =0.10.

(1): Productivity and C_RD; (2): Productivity and C_CAP;

(3) : C_ROA and Productivity; (4): C_ROA and C_RD;

(5) : C_ROA and C_CAP.

+ : Significant positive correlation;

- : Significant negative correlation.

Pre FASB: Without Implementation of FASB-94, Consolidation of ALL Majority-Owned Subsidiaries.

Research and Development Expenses and Profitability

The fourth hypothesis changes in research and development expenses are not related to profitability changes is rejected in 23 companies (i.e., 11 positive and 12 negative) at the 0.05 level and in 34 companies (i.e., 14 positive and 20 negative) at the 0.10 level as shown in Table 15. As Table 16 illustrates, 11 companies (i.e., 2 food, 2 paper, and 7 chemicals) with positive correlations and 12 companies (i.e., 1 food, 1 paper, 1 chemicals, 3 computer, 4 electronics, and 2 motor) with negative correlations are significant at the 0.05 level. Three companies (i.e., 1 paper and 2 chemicals) with positive correlations and eight companies (i.e., 2 food, 1 paper, 1 chemicals, 2 computer, and 2 electronics) with negative correlations are significant at the 0.10 level.

Capital Expenditures and Profitability

The fifth hypothesis—changes in capital expenditures are not related to profitability changes—is rejected in 11 companies (i.e., 5 positive and 6 negative) at the 0.05 level and in 15 companies (i.e., 7 positive and 8 negative) at the 0.10 level as shown in Table 15. As Table 16 reflects, 5 companies (i.e., 1 food, 3 chemicals, and 1 motor) with positive correlations and 6 companies (i.e., 2 food, 2 chemicals, 1 electronics, and 1 motor) with negative correlations at $\alpha = 0.05$. Two companies (i.e., 1 chemicals and 1 motor) with positive correlations and two other companies (i.e., 1 chemicals and 1 computer) with negative correlations are significant only at $\alpha = 0.10$.

Observations on One-Year Lag Relationships

Four companies have five positive relationships one year after the increase in investments. These four companies are Unilever N V, Imperial Chemicals, Abbott Laboratories, and Marion Merrell Dow. Kellogg Corporation has the same relationships as in the no lag analysis. Campbell Soup Corporation has the same two positive relationships and three negative relationships as Kellogg Corporation.

Two-Year Lag

The results of the tests of the same five hypotheses for two years after the pertinent expenditures are presented in Table 17. Companies with significant correlations are listed in Table 18 at two significance levels.

Table 17
Two-Year Lag: Five Major Relationships for 77 Companies

	Significant Positive Correlation		Significant Negative Correlation		Nonsignificant	
	5%	10%	5%	10%	5%	10%
Productivity and C_RD	25	28[*]	9	9	43	40
Productivity and C_CAP	12	14	6	6	59	57
C_ROA and Productivity	12	14	7	12	58	51
C_ROA and C_RD	15	18	11	15	51	44
C_ROA and C_CAP	5	9	8	12	64	56

Note: The number in each cell indicates the total number of industries in each category. Thus, the 28 companies with significance at the 0.10 level include the 25 companies with significance at the 0.05 level.

Table 18
Two-Year Lag: List of 77 Companies with Significant Correlations

SIC Code	Company Name	Relationship				
		(1)	(2)	(3)	(4)	(5)
2000	BORDEN INC	+				
2000	CAMPBELL SOUP CO	+	+	-	-	-
2000	UNILEVER PLC-AMER SHRS			+	+	
2000	UNILEVER N V-NY SHARES			+	+	+
2040	KELLOGG CO	+	+	-	-	-
2040	RALSTON PURINA CO	+				
2600	INTL PAPER CO	+		+	+	+*
2600	MEAD CORP					
2621	BOISE CASCADE CORP	+*			+*	
2621	DOMTAR INC			-*	-	-
2621	KIMBERLY-CLARK CORP	+		+	+	
2621	UNION CAMP CORP					-
2621	WESTVACO CORP	+				
2670	BEMIS CO			+		
2670	DENNISON MFG CO					
2670	NASHUA CORP			-*	-*	
2800	AMERICAN CYANAMID CO	+	+			
2800	ETHYL CORP	+				-*
2800	ETHYL CORP-PRE FASB	+		+	+	
2800	FMC CORP			-		
2800	FERRO CORP				+	

Notes: One asterisk (*) indicates significance only at $\alpha = 0.10$.
    (1): Productivity and C_RD; (2): Productivity and C_CAP;
    (3) : C_ROA and Productivity; (4): C_ROA and C RD;
    (5) : C_ROA and C CAP.
    + : Significant positive correlation;
    - : Significant negative correlation.
    Pre FASB: Without Implementation of FASB-94, Consolidation of
    ALL Majority-Owned Subsidiaries.

Table 18 (Continued)

Two-Year Lag: List of 77 Companies with Significant Correlations

SIC Code	Company Name	Relationship				
		(1)	(2)	(3)	(4)	(5)
2800	HERCULES INC					
2800	IMPERIAL CHEN INDS PLC-ADR		+			+*
2800	OLIN CORP					
2820	DU PONT (E.I.) DE NEMOURS	+		+	+	
2821	DEXTER CORP					
2821	GOODRICH (B.F.) CO					
2821	UNION CARBIDE CORP		-			
2834	ABBOTT LABORATORIES	+	+	+	+	+
2834	BAXTER INTERNATIONAL INC	-	-			
2834	BRISTOL MYERS SQUIBB	+				
2834	CARTER-WALLACE INC	+*		+	+	+
2834	FOREST LABORATORIES-CL A	-	-	-*	+	+*
2834	JOHNSON & JOHNSON	+				
2834	LILLY (ELI) & CO	+	+			
2834	MARION MERRELL DOW INC	+	+	+	+	+
2834	MYLAN LABORATORIES					
2834	WARNER-LAMBERT CO	+				
2840	CHEMED CORP					
2840	COLGATE-PALMOLIVE CO		+			
2840	PROCTER & GAMBLE CO	+	+			-*
2851	DE SOTO INC				-	
2851	PRG INDUSTRIES INC	+			+*	

Notes: One asterisk (*) indicates significance only at $\alpha = 0.10$.
   (1): Productivity and C_RD; (2): Productivity and C_CAP;
   (3) : C_ROA and Productivity; (4): C_ROA and C_RD;
   (5) : C_ROA and C_CAP.
   + : Significant positive correlation;
   - : Significant negative correlation.
   Pre FASB: Without Implementation of FASB-94, Consolidation of
   ALL Majority-Owned Subsidiaries.

Table 18 (Continued)
Two-Year Lag: List of 77 Companies with Significant Correlations

SIC Code	Company Name	Relationship				
		(1)	(2)	(3)	(4)	(5)
2851	PRATT & LAMBERT INC			-*	-*	
2851	SHERWIN-WILLIAMS INC	+		+	+*	
2890	BETZ LABORATORIES INC	+				
2890	LAWTER INTERNATIONAL INC					
2890	NALCO CHEMICAL CO			-		
3570	CONTROL DATA CORP	-	+*			
3570	DATA GENERAL CORP	+			-	-
3570	DIGITAL EQUIPMENT	+	+		+	
3570	HEWLETT-PACKARD CO					-*
3570	INTL BUSINESS MACHINES CORP	-		+	-	+*
3570	WANG LABORATORIES-CL B			-		
3571	COMMODORE INTL LTD	-		-		
3571	FLOATING POINT SYSTEMS INC	-			-	
3621	BALDOR ELECTRIC					
3621	EMERSON ELECTRIC CO			-	-*	
3621	KOLLMLRGEN CORP		-			
3621	VERNITRON CORP				-*	-
3663	ANDREW CORP	-			-	-*
3663	AYDIN CORP			-		
3663	GENERAL INSTRUMENT CORP					
3663	SCIENTIFIC-ATLANTA INC					
3670	CTS CORP			-*		

Notes: One asterisk (*) indicates significance only at $\alpha = 0.10$.
    (1): Productivity and C_RD; (2): Productivity and C_CAP;
    (3) : C_ROA and Productivity; (4): C_ROA and C_RD;
    (5) : C_ROA and C_CAP.
    + : Significant positive correlation;
    - : Significant negative correlation.
    Pre FASB: Without Implementation of FASB-94, Consolidation of ALL Majority-Owned Subsidiaries.

Table 18 (Continued)
Two-Year Lag: List of 77 Companies with Significant Correlations

SIC Code	Company Name	Relationship (1)	(2)	(3)	(4)	(5)
3670	VARTAN ASSOCIATES INC					
3674	ADVANCED MICRO DEVICES			-		-
3674	INTL RECTIFIER CORP					
3674	UNITRODE CORP	-		+*	-	
3711	FORD MOTOR CO	+	+*	+*	+	
3711	FORD MOTOR CO-PRE FASB	+*	+			
3711	GENERAL MOTOR CORP				+	
3711	GENERAL MOTOR CORP-PRE FASB				+	
3714	ECHLIN INC	-	-		-	-
3714	SMITH (A.O) CORP-CL A		-			+
3714	SPARTON CORP					
3714	STANDARD PRODUCTS CO	+	+			

Notes: One asterisk (*) indicates significance only at $\alpha = 0.10$.
      (1): Productivity and C_RD; (2): Productivity and C_CAP;
      (3) : C_ROA and Productivity; (4): C_ROA and C_RD;
      (5) : C_ROA and C_CAP.
      + : Significant positive correlation;
      - : Significant negative correlation.
      Pre FASB: Without Implementation of FASB-94, Consolidation of
      ALL Majority-Owned Subsidiaries.

Research and Development Expenses and Productivity

As shown in Table 17, the first hypothesis—changes in research and development expenses are not related to changes in productivity — is rejected in 34 (i.e., 25 positive and 9 negative) of the 77 companies at the 0.05 significance level and in 37 (i.e., 28 positive and 9 negative) of those companies at the 0.10 significance level; As Table 18 reflects, 25 companies (i.e., 4 food, 3 paper, 14 chemicals, 2 computer, and 2 motor) with positive correlations and 9 companies (i.e., 2 chemicals, 4 computer,

2 electronics, and 1 motor) with negative correlations are significant at the 0.05 level. Three companies (i.e., 1 paper, 1 chemicals, and 1 motor) with positive correlations are significant only at the 0.10 level.

Capital Expenditures and Productivity

The second hypothesis — changes in capital expenditures are not related to changes in productivity — is rejected in 18 companies (i.e., 12 positive and 6 negative) at the 0.05 level and in 20 companies (i.e., 14 positive and 6 negative) at the 0.10 level as shown in Table 17. As Table 18 illustrates, 12 companies (i.e., 2 food, 7 chemicals, 1 computer, and 2 motor) with positive correlations and 6 companies (i.e., 3 chemicals, 1 electronics, and 2 motor) with negative correlations are significant at the 0.05 level. Two companies (i.e., 1 computer and 1 motor) with positive correlations are significant only at the 0.10 level.

Productivity and Profitability

As presented in Table 17, the third hypothesis—productivity changes have no effect on profitability changes — is rejected in 19 companies (i.e., 12 positive and 7 negative) at the 0.05 level and in 26 companies (i.e., 14 positive and 12 negative) at the 0.10 level. As Table 18 reflects, 12 companies (i.e., 2 food, 3 paper, 6 chemicals, and 1 computer) with positive correlations and 7 companies (i.e., 2 food, 2 chemicals, and 3 electronics) with negative correlations are significant at $\alpha = 0.05$. Two companies (i.e., 1 electronics and 1 motor) with positive correlations and five companies (i.e., 2 paper, 2 chemicals, and 1 electronics) with negative correlations are significant only at $\alpha = 0.10$.

Research and Development Expenses and Profitability

The fourth hypothesis — changes in research and development expenses are not related to profitability changes — is rejected in 26 companies (i.e., 15 positive and 11 negative) at the 0.05 level and in 33 companies (i.e., 18 positive and 15 negative) at the 0.10 level as shown in Table 17. As Table 18 indicates, 15 companies (i.e., 2 food, 2 paper, 7 chemicals, 1 computer, and 3 motor) with positive correlations and 11 companies (i.e., 2 food, 1 paper, 1 chemicals, 4 computer, 2 electronics, and 1 motor) with negative correlations are significant at the 0.05 level. Three companies (i.e., 1 paper and 2 chemicals) with positive correlations and four companies (i.e., 1 paper, 1 chemicals, and 2 electronics) with negative correlations are significant only at the 0.10 level.

Capital Expenditures and Profitability

The fifth hypothesis—changes in capital expenditures are not related to profitability changes—is rejected in 13 companies (i.e., 5 positive and 8 negative) at the 0.05 level and in 21 companies (i.e., 9 positive and 12 negative) at the 0.10 level as presented in Table 17. As Table 18 reflects, the results are significant for 5 companies (i.e., 1 food, 3 chemicals, and 1 motor) with positive correlations and 8 companies (i.e., 2 food, 2 paper, 1 computer, 2 electronics, and 1 motor) with negative correlations at a=0.05. Four companies (i.e., 1 paper, 2 chemicals, and 1 computer) with positive correlations and four other companies (i.e., 2 chemicals, 1 computer, and 1 electronics) with negative correlations are significant only at α =0.10.

Observations on Two-Year Lag Relationships

Abbott Laboratories Corporation and Marion Merrell Dow Corporation have five positive relationships for all three years. Campbell Soups and Kellogg have the same two positive relationships and three negative relationships as reported above. Otherwise, none of the 77 companies reflected five relationships that endured at significant levels throughout the three-year time frame of analysis in this study.

Summary Observations on Company Relationships

The results of the tests of the five hypothesized relationships at the company level show that at least one of the five relationships is significant in the great majority of the 77 sample companies during the 1980-1989 period. Only three companies (i.e., Dennison Mfg., Olin, and Goodrich) show no significant relationships in any of the three time periods that are analyzed. In practice, manufacturing companies expect positive relationships so that the benefits of investments can be realized in the investment year and/or in future periods. However, negative relationships may occasionally result from ineffective investments.

The findings reveal that the benefits of some investments are realized in a short time period. For example, changes in catalyst financial commitments have immediately positive impacts on productivity in paper companies, and productivity changes have positive effects on profitability in the investment year in both computer and electric companies. In other companies, benefits of investments are realized in the year of investment and one year after. For instance, changes in catalyst financial commitments have positive impacts on productivity in food companies. According to the literature, many companies in this industry have made substantial investments in developing new products to satisfy changes in customers' tastes

Of most interest in this study, however, are the remaining companies where significant relationships between changes in catalyst financial commitments and productivity/profitability changes are identified for all three periods. As shown in Table 19, ten companies have three or more significant relationships for all three periods (i.e., no lag, one-year lag, and two-year lag). Four companies — Ethyl-Pre FASB, DuPont, Sherwin-Williams, and Unilever N V—have three positive relationships in the study period. IBM has two negative relationships and one positive relationship, while Echlin has three negative relationships. In addition, four positive relationships are significant in the Carter-Wallace Corporation. Finally, two companies—Abbott Laboratories and Marion Merrell Dow—have five significant positive relationships for all three periods.

Table 19
Significant Relationships for Three Periods
in Selected Companies

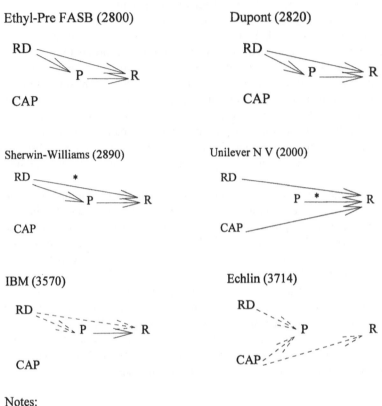

Ethyl-Pre FASB (2800)

Dupont (2820)

Sherwin-Williams (2890)

Unilever N V (2000)

IBM (3570)

Echlin (3714)

Notes:
" ___ " positive relationship; "_ _ _":Negative relationship.
RD: changes in R&D; CAP:changes in capital expenditures;
P:productivity; R:changes in return on asset.
"*" : significance only at the 0.10 level.
Pre FASB: without implementation of FASB-94, Consolidation of
All Majority-Owned Subsidiaries.

Table 19 (Continued)
Significant Relationships for Three Periods
in Selected Companies

Carter-Wallace (2834)

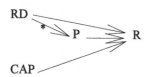

Kellogg (2000)

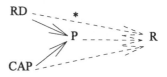

Abbott Laboratories (2834)

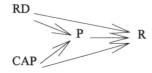

Marion Merrell Dow (2834)

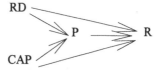

Notes:

"____" " positive relationship; "_ _ _":Negative relationship.
RD: changes in R&D; CAP:changes in capital expenditures;
P:productivity; R:changes in return on asset.
"*" : significance only at the 0.10 level.
Pre FASB: without implementation of FASB-94, Consolidation of
All Majority-Owned Subsidiaries.

As reflected in the diagrams in Table 19, the findings show that four companies have a similar pattern of relationships. Ethyl-Pre FASB and DuPont have the same three relationships at the 0.05 significance level. Sherwin-Williams also has the same relationships, but one relationship is significant only at the 0.10 level. For IBM, two of the relationships are significantly negative, and only one is significantly positive. These results may reflect the fact that investments in research and development projects to produce new computer products are risky because new ·computer systems may not be purchased by consumers to replace their old systems.

Similarly, Kellogg, Abbott Laboratories, and Marion Merrell Dow share a pattern of relationships. In Abbott Laboratories and Marion Merrell Dow, all five relationships are significantly positive at the 0.05 level. Since the pharmaceutical industry is a high-profit industry, these companies can increase their profits once they make wise investments in new product development to increase sales and in better equipment to reduce manufacturing expenses. However, three of the five relationships are significantly negative in Kellogg. These results may reflect incorrect predictions about their customers' tastes; also possible, of course, is that some of the negative relationships result from ineffective management practices. Ideally, future field studies can provide improved insights into the cause/effect dimensions underlying findings in this exploratory study.

SUMMARY

This chapter has presented the results of this study with respect to the five major relationships at both the industry level and the company level. Time lag results were discussed at both levels. The results show that five major relationships do exist in several companies.

The next chapter is devoted to most useful findings, conclusions, and suggested areas for the future research. With respect to future research studies, many distinguishable possibilities exist. As will be seen, however, emphasis is placed on industries and companies that were highlighted in the profile of significant relationships sections presented in this chapter.

VI

Conclusions and Suggestion

An overall summary of this study and observations based on the analysis of the findings are presented in this chapter. The first part of the chapter is a brief overview of the study. The second section indicates assumptions and limitations of the study. The third part summarizes the most useful findings. Conclusions and recommendations as to areas that may be deserving of future research are suggested in the last section.

SUMMARY OBSERVATIONS

The primary objective of this study was to explore possible relationships between changes in catalyst financial commitments (i.e., research and development projects and capital improvements) and changes in productivity and profitability, as well as relationships between productivity changes and profitability changes, in selected manufacturing industries and companies. Specific attention was focused on empirically investigating the impact of increased catalyst financial commitments on changes in productivity and profitability. In seeking to determine the effects of substantial investments, this study has the following research objectives:

1. To investigate the impacts of changes in catalyst financial commitments on productivity changes.
2. To determine whether there are significant relationships between productivity changes and profitability changes.
3. To examine the impacts of increases in research and development expenses and capital expenditures on profitability changes.
4. To investigate the existence of time lags between changes in substantial investments and productivity/profitability changes for the first and the second year after the year of investment.

To accomplish these research objectives, this study reviews the relevant literature from both the economics and the management accounting perspectives. The economics literature shows clearly that economic growth in the United States has declined dramatically since 1973. Thus, research on productivity at the national level has increased along with increased public interest in economic growth. Some studies imply that economic growth can be improved by investments in research and development projects and capital improvements, these commitments, in turn, can lead to technological innovations that result in increased productivity. Kendrick's studies have made a major contribution by bringing productivity measurement from the national level to the industry level.

Due to rapid changes in the world-wide manufacturing environment, American companies have been forced to maintain or improve the quality of their goods at lower costs in order to be able to compete with foreign companies in the international markets. Many U.S. manufacturers have increased their investments in research and development projects and capital improvements in order to achieve these goals. Since these investments are fundamental to a firm's survival, this study investigates the impacts of increases in catalyst financial commitments on changes in productivity and profitability.

To accomplish the objectives of this study, five hypotheses are tested for each subgroup (i.e., industry and company) of the sample as follows:

H_{01} : Changes in Research and Development Expenses are not related to Productivity changes.

H_{02} : Changes in Capital Expenditures are not related to Productivity changes.

H_{03} : Productivity changes are not related to Profitability changes.

H_{04} : Changes in Research and Development Expenses are not related to Profitability changes.

H_{05} : Changes in Capital Expenditures are not related to Profitability changes.

The research methodology for this study is based on a combination of library research and empirical research. The library research synthesizes the relevant literature on the selection of productivity measurement models. A frequently used model for measuring productivity changes created by the American Productivity Center is used in this study. The empirical research utilizes relevant data from a publicly available database, the COMPUSTAT II files, and the time frame of this research is the ten-year period 1980-1989.

For the purpose of this study, companies with substantial research and development and capital expenditures are included in the sample, after other industry and company selection criteria are satisfied. Four industry selection criteria are used: (1) type of industry, (2) annual amount of Research and Development Expenses, (3) annual amount of Capital Expenditures, and (4) capacity utilization rate. Since this study focuses on empirical analysis of the five relationships in the U.S. manufacturing sector, only manufacturing industries are included in the sample. To select industries with substantial investments, an industry-wide average annual amount in excess of $10 million is used as a requirement for both research and development expenses and capital expenditures. The capacity utilization rate is used to select industries that have average annual capacity utilization rates above that of their subgroup.

Four company selection criteria are: (1) annual amount of Research and Development Expenses, (2) annual amount of Capital Expenditures, and (3) availability of complete 10-year data, and (4) no change in inventory valuation methods during the 1980-1989 period. For the selected companies both the mean of annual research and development expenses and the mean of annual capital expenditures for the 10-year period are greater than $1 million. In addition, only companies with complete 10-year data for each variable are selected for the sample. To remove the possible effect of changes in inventory valuation methods on two performance measures (i.e., productivity and profitability), companies with any change in inventory valuation methods during the study period are not included in this study. As a result, the research sample comprises 77 companies in 20 manufacturing industries.

Five major relationships among four variables (i.e., C_RD, C_CAP, PRODUCTIVITY, and C_ROA) are examined at the industry level and at the company level. Correlation analysis is used to measure the direction and strength of the relationships between various pairs of the variables. In addition, this study investigates time lags between increases in catalyst financial commitments and changes in productivity and profitability.

ASSUMPTIONS AND LIMITATIONS OF THE STUDY

Four primary assumptions are used in this study. The first assumption is that the productivity model created by the American Productivity Center (APC) is generally applicable to all manufacturing companies. The APC productivity model is an improved measure of changes in productivity. Two variables in this APC model are sales and cost of goods sold. The second assumption is that publicly available and accessible data can be as effective for this type of productivity and profitability analysis as internally developed data.

The third assumption is that the Producer Price Index published by the Department of Labor is appropriate for deflating measures of sales and cost of goods sold in each year of the study to the base year. The fourth assumption is that industries with capacity utilization rates above the average annual capacity utilization rate for its subgroup (nondurable or durable goods industries) are considered to be effectively and efficiently operating industries.

This study is limited in scope and methodology. In terms of scope, the COMPUSTAT II files are used as the database. Therefore, the sample of this study is limited to the companies in this database. The COMPUSTAT II files include only 2,478 companies in 382 industries. Consequently, conclusions drawn from the findings of this study can be applied only to companies included in these files. Note further that a narrowly defined industry construct is used in this study; consequently, not all companies that could have been included in industry analyses were considered for these purposes. Also relevant is that only those manufacturing industries with above-average capacity utilization and companies with substantial catalyst financial commitments are included in this study. In addition, the time frame is limited to the ten-year period 1980-1989. Furthermore, the investigation of time lags between substantial investments and resulting benefits is limited to the investment year and two succeeding years.

In terms of methodology, the productivity model created by the American Productivity Center is used to measure the productivity of the selected companies because the data needed for this model can be obtained through publicly available data. As indicated in the cited literature, a limitation of the APC model is its assumption of a constant product mix between periods. Also noted as a limitation is that the relevant profitability measure (i.e., Return on Assets) is not inflation-adjusted.

THE MOST USEFUL FINDINGS

The findings of this study are reported in Chapter Five where the results are tabulated and discussed. This section reiterates the primary findings in summary form. The five major relationships are discussed at both industry and company levels. The results are examined at these two levels for the year of investment and for time lags in each of the two succeeding years.

Significant Relationships in Selected Industries

The selected 77 companies in 20 industries are used in the five relationship analysis at the industry level. Relationships between changes in research and development expenses and productivity changes, as well as relationships between productivity changes and profitability changes, are significant throughout all three periods (i.e., no lag, one-year lag, and two-year lag) in many industries. Profiles of these relationships were presented in summary form in Table 12 (Chapter Five).

One or more relationships exist in ten industries for all three periods in the sample. Six industries show one significant relationship for all three periods. The first relationship — changes in research and development expenses are related to productivity changes — exists in the soap and detergent industry and the electronic computer industry. However, changes in research and development expenses have negative effects on productivity in the electronic computer industry. The second relationship — changes in capital expenditures are related to productivity changes—exists in two industries (i.e., miscellaneous chemicals and computer and office equipment). The third relationship — productivity changes are related to profitability changes—exists in the food and kindred products industry and the motors and generators industry.

The paper and allied products industry and the pharmaceutical preparations industry have two significant positive relationships for all three periods. In the paper and allied products industry increased investment in research and development improves productivity, and in addition productivity increases have positive effects on profitability (i.e., the first and third relationships, respectively). The fourth and fifth relationships in the Study Focus Model for this study — changes in research and development expenses and capital expenditures are related to profitability changes — exist for all three periods in the pharmaceutical preparations industry.

Finally, three positive relationships exist in the paper mills industry and in the plastic materials industry. Increases in research and development improve productivity and profitability, and productivity changes increase profitability in these two industries. These ten industries with significant relationships for all three periods indicate the existence of time lags between changes in catalyst financial commitments and changes in productivity and profitability.

Significant Relationships in Selected Companies

The same hypotheses are tested at the company level. Results show that relationships between changes in research and development expenses and productivity changes and relationships between productivity changes and profitability changes exist throughout three periods in many companies. Profiles of these relationships were presented in summary form in Table 19 (Chapter Five).

Three positive relationships exist in four companies. Increases in research and development expenses improve productivity and profitability and productivity changes have positive effects on profitability in three of these companies (i.e., Ethyl-Pre FASB, DuPont, and Sherwin Williams). Three other relationships exist in Unilever Company: profitability is improved by increases in productivity and investments in research and development projects and capital improvements. In contrast, three negative relationships exist in Echlin Corporation for all three periods. Changes in each of the catalyst investments decrease productivity, and changes in capital expenditures also decrease profitability in this company. For IBM, the results are mixed: increases in research and development expenses have negative effects on both productivity and profitability, while productivity increases have positive effects on profitability.

One company, Carter-Wallace, shows four positive relationships for the year of increased investment and the succeeding two years. In this company, productivity is improved by increases in investments in research and development projects. Also, profitability is improved by increases in productivity and in the catalyst financial commitments.

Five relationships exist in three companies—Kellogg, Abbott Laboratories, and Marion Merrell Dow — for all three periods. Kellogg Corporation has two positive relationships and three negative relationships. Increases in the catalyst financial commitments improve productivity, but increases in productivity and investments in research and development projects and capital improvements have negative impacts on profitability in this food company. Also of interest, two companies, Abbott Laboratories and Marion Merrell Dow, have five significantly positive relationships for all three periods. Further analysis reveals that these two companies both have positive amounts of net operating income in each of the ten years examined during this study.

Summary on Major Relationships

Ideally, increases in catalyst financial commitments are expected to improve productivity and/or profitability. The benefits of substantial investments can be realized immediately and/or in future periods. For example, benefits are realized in the short term in both food industries (i.e., food and kindred products and grain mill products), but benefits are realized in future periods in the motor vehicles industry. In other cases, the findings reveal the existence of negative relationships between investments and benefits. The negative relationships may result from several causes (i.e., ineffective investment decisions and management practices, or, perhaps even statistical errors in those cases where measurement differences were of only small magnitude). For instance, computer companies have had losses for several years when their new products were not popular in the market. Examining these findings in more depth may eventually allow a clearer understanding of relationships between investments and benefits in both companies and their related industry groupings.

STUDY CONCLUSIONS

The incidence of positive relationships — both in industries and in companies — indicates that catalyst financial commitments (i.e., research and development and capital improvements) are yielding substantial benefits in the U.S. manufacturing environment. Industries with multiple positive relationships offer opportunities (i.e., through survey research methods) for obtaining added insights into non-financial variables that offset benefits derived from catalyst commitments. Companies with multiple positive relationships should be analyzed in added depth through uses of more powerful research techniques (e.g., regression models, field study, etc.). Together, these expanded analyses should provide a useful foundation for improved planning and control models.

While exploratory investigations using correlation analysis provide useful insights, this approach provides only a starting point. Industry studies must proceed, perhaps by survey research techniques, to examine more carefully the impacts of other variables as defined in Figure 4 (Major Relationships in the Gold Model Chapter Five). Company studies, on the other hand, should proceed by using field study techniques. In this way, findings about other impacting industry variables can be examined with the assistance of knowledgeable industry executives. These combined efforts of management accountants from the academic and practice environments should serve most effectively to improve available planning and control models throughout the manufacturing environment.

This study, in its present form, and with further refinements as well, can prove useful to researchers who are interested in exploring international manufacturing environments. As a first step, of course, the informational resources (i.e., publicly available databases) in other countries must be examined. Then, ideally the same sets of relationships can be examined to provide added insights into the impacts of catalyst financial commitments on productivity/profitability performance in these countries. Ultimately, of course, improved planning and control models should also be possible in both developed and underdeveloped countries throughout the world.

SUGGESTED AREAS FOR FUTURE RESEARCH

The major findings of this study show that productivity and profitability can be improved by investments in research and development projects and capital improvements. However, the findings also reveal the existence of negative relationships in the sample. Both sets of findings are sufficiently interesting to warrant further research investigations.

At the industry level, for example, survey research can be used to investigate factors that led to positive relationships between changes in research and development expenses and changes in productivity in the soap and detergent industry but a negative relationship in the electronic computer industry. Clearly, as discussed previously, many factors could conceivably contribute to these results. Additional perspectives about these factors must be identified if further studies are to be more effective.

Analyses of relationships in this study are purposefully restricted to three time frames: no lag, one-year lag, and two-year lag periods. In practice, time lags between changes in substantial investments and changes in productivity and profitability may be longer than two years. Therefore, time lags can be extended to three or more years to determine whether longer periods of lags between investments and results are prevalent in various industries. As a complement to future industry analyses, field studies can prove useful to investigate both significant positive relationships in companies (e.g., Abbott Laboratories, Marion Merrell Dow, etc.) and significant negative relationships as well (e.g., IBM, Echlin, Kellogg, etc.).

In addition, the APC productivity model used in this study can be applied to companies that do not have substantial investments in research and development and capital expenditures. Performances of the companies in this study can be compared with those of other companies to determine whether substantial investments in catalyst financial commitments lead to higher performance levels in terms of productivity and/or profitability. Such comparisons can also be useful as future international accounting research studies are conducted. In this way, insights into factors contributing to improved productivity and profitability in the developed countries may ultimately be used to assist efforts by third-world countries to improve their performance.

Since the results of this study show the existence of the five major relationships in the U.S. manufacturing sector, the same five null hypotheses can be tested in manufacturing sectors within other countries. The industries with the greatest number of significant relationships can be identified to determine differences between countries. Then, reasons for these differences can be investigated empirically, and perhaps through applications of more advanced statistical techniques as well. These results should provide bases for improved international investment planning and control efforts.

For productivity and profitability comparisons in different countries, more powerful statistical analyses of industry and company relationships may also provide many useful insights. For instance, the performance of the computer and office industry in Taiwan can be compared with that of this same industry in the United States. Comparisons of similar companies should also prove useful. Since this is a high-technology industry in Taiwan, that country's government offers investment tax credits to computer companies to encourage them to make commitments for new projects relating to technological innovations. Evaluating the impacts of such tax incentives on each of this study's five relationships may offer useful perspectives about alternative tax policies.

Additional analyses reveal that 46 of the 77 companies had positive amounts of net operating income in each year during the 1980-1989 study period. This finding suggests that the five relationships for companies with income in each of the years are more significant than those of companies with losses in some of the years. Of most interest, however, are the changes in results that occur when the companies with some years of losses are eliminated from the original 77-company sample. The five relationships for these 46 companies during the three periods are shown in Appendices 3-4-5. Comparing results in these three appendices with results in Tables 13, 15, and 17 (Chapter Five), the number of companies in the nonsignificant category decreases dramatically. This difference has implications for sample selection in future studies.

Another possible future study would use different input measures for the variable labeled "catalyst financial commitments." Specifically, this study uses dollar amounts of research and development expenses and capital expenditures as the input variable. Changes in ratios could also be used as input measures. For example, Appendices 6-7-8 offer results based on two new input measures: (1) changes in the ratio of research and development expenses to net operating income, and (2) changes in the ratio of capital expenditures to total assets.

Finally, the focus of this study could be modified dramatically by shifting from income-based measures to changes in cash outlays for research and development projects and capital improvements. According to Statement No. 95 promulgated by the Financial Accounting Standards Board, American companies are required to prepare a Statement of Cash Flows in their financial statements for fiscal years ending on or after July 16, 1988. Information on cash outlays for research and development projects and capital improvements should thus be available in the 1990s. In the coming decade, therefore, these five relationships could be examined in a completely different context.

This exploratory study reveals clearly that relationships between changes in catalyst financial commitments and changes in productivity and profitability are deserving of further empirical research attention. The findings, when extended and refined, should prove useful in developing improved planning and control models for management accountants in the practice, both within the U.S. and perhaps in international settings as well. Given this foundation, efforts to improve productivity and profitability in the new manufacturing environment should continue to be effective throughout the 1990s and into the twenty-first century.

Appendices

SIC Code	Industry Name	No. of Companies
2000	FOOD AND KINDRED PRODUCTS	4
2040	GRAIN MILL PRODUCTS	2
2600	PAPER AND ALLIED PRODUCTS	2
2621	PAPER MILLS	5
2670	CONVER PAPR, PAPRBRD,EX BOXES	3
2800	CHEMICALS & ALLIED PRODS	8
2820	PLASTIC MATL, SYSTHETIC RESIN	1
2821	PLASTICS,RESINS, ELASTOMERS	3
2834	PHARMACEUTICAL PREPARATIONS	10
2840	SOAP,DETERGENT, TOILET,P PREPS	3
2851	PAINTS,VARNISHES, LACQUERS	4
2890	MISC CHEMICAL PRODUCTS	3
3570	COMPUTER & OFFICE EQUIPMENT	2
3571	ELECTRONIC COMPUTERS	2
3621	MOTORS AND GENERATORS	4
3663	RADIO, TV BROADCAST, COMM EQ	4
3670	ELECTRONIC COMP, ACCESSORIES	2
3674	SEMICONDUCTOR, RELATED DEVICE	3
3711	MOTOR VEHICLES & CAR BODIES	4
3714	MOTOR VEHICLE PART, ACCESSORY	4

Total 20 Industries   77 Companies

Appendix 2
List of 77 Companies

SIC Code	Industry Name	Company Name
2000	FOOD AND KINDRED PRODUCTS	BORDEN INC
2000	FOOD AND KINDRED PRODUCTS	CAMPBELL SOUP CO
2000	FOOD AND KINDRED PRODUCTS	UNILEVER PLC-AMER SHRS
2000	FOOD AND KINDRED PRODUCTS	UNILEVER N V-NY SHARES
2040	GRAIN MILL PRODUCTS	KELLOGG CO
2040	GRAIN MILL PRODUCTS	RALSTON PURINA CO
2600	PAPER AND ALLIED PRODUCTS	INTL PAPER CO
2600	PAPER AND ALLIED PRODUCTS	MEAD CORP
2621	PAPER MILLS	BOISE CASCADE CORP
2621	PAPER MILLS	DOMTAR INC
2621	PAPER MILLS	KIMBERLY-CLARK CORP
2621	PAPER MILLS	UNION CAMP CORP
2621	PAPER MILLS	WESTVACO CORP
2670	CONVRT PAPR,PAPRBRD,EX,BOXES	BEMIS CO
2670	CONVRT PAPR,PAPRBRD,EX,BOXES	DENNISON MFG CO
2670	CONVRT PAPR,PAPRBRD,EX,BOXES	NASHUA CORP
2800	CHEMICALS & ALLIED PRODS	AMERICAN CYANAMID CO
2800	CHEMICALS & ALLIED PRODS	ETHYL CORP
2800	CHEMICALS & ALLIED PRODS	ETHYL CORP-PRE FASB
2800	CHEMICALS & ALLIED PRODS	FMC CORP
2800	CHEMICALS & ALLIED PRODS	FERRO CORP
2800	CHEMICALS & ALLIED PRODS	HERCULES INC
2800	CHEMICALS & ALLIED PRODS	IMPERIAL CHEM INDS PLC-ADR
2800	CHEMICALS & ALLIED PRODS	OLIN CORP
2821	PLASTICS,RESINS,ELASTOMERS	DU PONT (E.I.) DE NEMOURS
2821	PLASTICS,RESINS,ELASTOMERS	DEXTER CORP
2821	PLASTICS,RESINS,ELASTOMERS	GOODRICH (B.F.) CO
2821	PLASTICS,RESINS,ELASTOMERS	UNION CARBIDE CORP
2834	PHARMACEUTICAL PREPARATIONS	ABBOTT LABORATORIES

PRE FASB : Without Implementation of FASB-94, Consolidation of All Majority-Owned Subsidiaries, effective for financial statements covering fiscal years ending on or after December 16, 1988.

Appendix 2 (continued)
List of 77 Companies

SIC Code	Industry Name	Company Name
2834	PHARMACEUTICAL PREPARATIONS	BAXTER INTERNATIONAL INC
2834	PHARMACEUTICAL PREPARATIONS	BRISTOR MYERS SQUIBB
2834	PHARMACEUTICAL PREPARATIONS	CARTER-WALLACE INC
2834	PHARMACEUTICAL PREPARATIONS	FOREST LABORATORIES - CLA
2834	PHARMACEUTICAL PREPARATIONS	JOHNSON & JOHNSON
2834	PHARMACEUTICAL PREPARATIONS	LILLY (ELI) & CO
2834	PHARMACEUTICAL PREPARATIONS	MARION MERRELL DOW INC
2834	PHARMACEUTICAL PREPARATIONS	MYLAN LABORATORIES
2834	PHARMACEUTICAL PREPARATIONS	WARNER-LAMBERT CO
2840	SOAP,DETERGENT,TOILET PREPS	CHEMED CORP
2840	SOAP,DETERGENT,TOILET PREPS	COLGATE-PALMOLIVE CO
2840	SOAP,DETERGENT,TOILET PREPS	PROCTER & GAMBLE CO
2851	PAINTS,VARNISHES,LACQUERS	DE SOTO INC
2851	PAINTS,VARNISHES,LACQUERS	PRG INDUSTRIES INC
2851	PAINTS,VARNISHES,LACQUERS	PRATT & LAMBERT INC
2851	PAINTS,VARNISHES,LACQUERS	SHERWIN-WILLIAMS CO
2890	MISC CHEMICAL PRODUCTS	BETZ LABORATORIES INC
2890	MISC CHEMICAL PRODUCTS	LAWTER INTERNATIONAL INC
2890	MISC CHEMICAL PRODUCTS	NALCO CHEMICAL CO
3570	COMPUTER & OFFICE EQUIPMENT	CONTROL DATA CORP
3570	COMPUTER & OFFICE EQUIPMENT	DATA GENERAL CORP
3570	COMPUTER & OFFICE EQUIPMENT	DIGITAL EQUIPMENT
3570	COMPUTER & OFFICE EQUIPMENT	HEWLETT-PACKARD CO
3570	COMPUTER & OFFICE EQUIPMENT	INTL BUSINESS MACHINES CORP
3570	COMPUTER & OFFICE EQUIPMENT	WANG LABORATORIES-CLB

PRE FASB : Without Implementation of FASB-94, Consolidation of All Majority-Owned Subsidiaries, effective for financial statements covering fiscal years ending on or after December 16, 1988.

Appendix 2 (continued)
List of 77 Companies

SIC Code	Industry Name	Company Name
3571	ELECTRONIC COMPUTERS	COMMODORE INTL LTD
3571	ELECTRONIC COMPUTERS	FLOATING POINT SYSTEMS INC
3621	MOTORS AND GENERATORS	BALDOR ELECTRIC
3621	MOTORS AND GENERATORS	EMERSON ELECTRIC CO
3621	MOTORS AND GENERATORS	KOLLMORGEN CORP
3621	MOTORS AND GENERATORS	VERNITRON CORP
3663	RADIO,TV BROADCAST, COMM EQ	ANDREW CORP
3663	RADIO,TV BROADCAST, COMM EQ	ANDIN CORP
3663	RADIO,TV BROADCAST, COMM EQ	GENERAL INSTRUMENT CORP
3663	RADIO,TV BROADCAST, COMM EQ	SCIENTIFIC-ATLANTA INC
3670	ELECTRONIC COMP,ACCESSORIES	CTS CORP
3670	ELECTRONIC COMP,ACCESSORIES	VARIAN ASSOCIATES INC
3674	SEMICONDUCTOR,RELATED DEVICE	ADVANCED MICRO DEVICES
3674	SEMICONDUCTOR,RELATED DEVICE	INTL RECTIFIER CORP
3674	SEMICONDUCTOR,RELATED DEVICE	UNITRODE CORP
3711	MOTOR VEHICLES & CAR BODIES	FORD MOTOR CO
3711	MOTOR VEHICLES & CAR BODIES	FORD MOTOR CO-PRE FASB
3711	MOTOR VEHICLES & CAR BODIES	GENERAL MOTORS CORP
3711	MOTOR VEHICLES & CAR BODIES	GENERAL MOTORS CORP-
3714	MOTOR VEHICLE PART, ACCESSORY	ECHLIN INC
3714	MOTOR VEHICLE PART, ACCESSORY	SMITH (A.O.) CORP -CLA
3714	MOTOR VEHICLE PART, ACCESSORY	SPARTON CORP
3714	MOTOR VEHICLE PART, ACCESSORY	STANDARD PRODUCTS CO

PRE FASB : Without Implementation of FASB-94, Consolidation of All Majority-Owned Subsidiaries, effective for financial statements covering fiscal years ending on or after December 16, 1988.

Appendix 3
No Lag: Five Major Relationships for 20 Companies

	Significant Positive Correlation		Significant Negative Correlation		Nonsignificant	
	5%	10%	5%	10%	5%	10%
Productivity and C_RD	28	30[*]	4	4	14	12
Productivity and C_CAP	14	21	4	4	28	21
C_ROA and Productivity	18	22	2	3	26	21
C_ROA and C_RD	12	13	3	7	31	26
C_ROA and C_CAP	8	11	4	5	34	30

Note: The number in each cell indicates the total number of industries in each category. Thus, the 30 companies with significance at the 0.10 level include the 28 companies with significance at the 0.05 level.

Appendix 4
One-Year Lag: Five Major Relationships for 46 Companies

	Significant Positive Correlation		Significant Negative Correlation		Nonsignificant	
	5%	10%	5%	10%	5%	10%
Productivity and C_RD	25	27*	4	4	17	15
Productivity and C_CAP	15	16	0	0	27	26
C_ROA and Productivity	14	17	2	5	30	24
C_ROA and C_RD	11	14	5	9	30	23
C_ROA and C_CAP	4	5	5	7	37	34

Note: The number in each cell indicates the total number of industries in each category. Thus, the 27 companies with significance at the 0.10 level include the 25 companies with significance at the 0.05 level.

Appendix 5
Two-Year Lag: Five Major Relationships for 46 Companies

	Significant Positive Correlation		Significant Negative Correlation		Nonsignificant	
	5%	10%	5%	10%	5%	10%
Productivity and C_RD	20	22[*]	5	5	21	19
Productivity and C_CAP	10	10	3	3	33	33
C_ROA and Productivity	12	12	6	9	28	23
C_ROA and C_RD	12	15	6	8	28	23
C_ROA and C_CAP	4	8	5	9	37	29

Note: The number in each cell indicates the total number of industries in each category. Thus, the 22 companies with significance at the 0.10 level include the 20 companies with significance at the 0.05 level.

Appendix 6
No Lag: Five Major Relationships for 46 Companies

	Significant Positive Correlation		Significant Negative Correlation		Nonsignificant	
	5%	10%	5%	10%	5%	10%
Productivity and C_RD	5	7[*]	12	13	29	26
Productivity and C_CAP	4	6	2	6	40	36
C_ROA and Productivity	18	22	2	3	26	21
C_ROA and C_RDI	1	1	34	35	11	10
C_ROA and C_CAT	6	8	5	5	35	33

Note: The number in each cell indicates the total number of industries in each category. Thus, the 7 companies with significance at the 0.10 level include the 5 companies with significance at the 0.05 level.

Appendix 7

One-Year Lag: Five Major Relationships for 46 Companies

	Significant Positive Correlation		Significant Negative Correlation		Nonsignificant	
	5%	10%	5%	10%	5%	10%
Productivity and C_RDI1	6	9[*]	6	7	34	30
Productivity and C_CAT1	6	11	1	2	39	33
C_ROA and Productivity 1	14	17	2	5	30	24
C_ROA and C_RDI1	2	2	9	13	35	31
C_ROA and C_CAT1	3	4	2	3	41	39

Note: The number in each cell indicates the total number of industries in each category. Thus, the 9 companies with significance at the 0.10 level include the 6 companies with significance at the 0.05 level.

Appendix 8
Two-Year Lag: Five Major Relationships for 46 Companies

	Significant Positive Correlation		Significant Negative Correlation		Nonsignificant	
	5%	10%	5%	10%	5%	10%
Productivity and C_RDI2	4	6*	5	5	37	35
Productivity and C_CAT2	6	9	1	2	39	35
C_ROA and Productivity2	12	12	6	9	˙ 28	25
C_ROA and C_RDI2	4	4	5	7	37	35
C_ROA and C_CAT2	3	3	4	8	39	35

Note: The number in each cell indicates the total number of industries in each category. Thus, the 6 companies with significance at the 0.10 level include the 4 companies with significance at the 0.05 level.

Annotated Bibliography

Ballen, Kate, "The New Look of Capital Spending," *Fortune* (March 1989), pp.115-120.

Banker, Rajiv D., Srikant M. Datar, and Robert S. Kaplan, "Productivity Measurement and Management Accounting," *Journal of Accounting Auditing & Finance* (Fall 1989), pp.528-554.

Bao, Ben-Hsien, and Da-Hsien Bao, "An Empirical Investigation of the Association Between Productivity and Firm Value," *Journal of Business Finance & Accounting* (Winter 1989), pp.699-717.

Bauer, Paul W., and Mary E. Deily, "A User's Guide to Capacity Utilization Measures," *Economic Commentary* (July 1988), pp. 1-4.

Baumol, William J., and Kenneth Mclennan, *Productivity Growth and U.S. Competitiveness*, New York : Oxford University Press, a Supplementary Paper of the Committee for Economic Development, 1985.

_____. Blockman, and Wolff, *Productivity and American Leadership*, Massachusetts : The MIT Press, 1989.

Belcher, John G, *The Productivity Management Process*, Houston : American Productivity Center, 1984.

Berndt, Ernst R., and Melvyn A. Fuss, *Productivity Measurement Using Capital Asset Valuation to Adjust for Variations in Utilization*, Washington, D.C. : Department of Energy, 1981.

_____. and Dieter M. Hesse, "Measuring and Assessing Capacity Utilization in the Manufacturing Sectors of Nine OECD Counties," *European Economic Review* (October 1986), pp. 961-989.

Brayton, Gary N, "Productivity Measure Aids in Profit Analysis," *Management Accounting* (January 1985), pp. 54-58.

Bromwich, Michael, and Al Bhimani, "Strategic Investment Appraisal," *Management Accounting* (March 1991), pp. 45-48.

Brownstein, Vivian, "The Urge for New Equipment Will Keep Business Investment Growing," *Fortune* (December 1989), pp. 33-36.

Buzzell, Robert D., and Bradley T. Gale, *The PIMS Principles*, New York : The Free Press, 1987.

Cobb, Charies W., and Paul H. Douglas, "A Theory of Production," *American Economic Review* (1928), pp. 139-165.

Craig, Charies E., and R. Clark Harris, "Total Productivity Measurement at the Firm Level," *Sloan Management Review* (Spring 1973), pp. 13-29.

Davis, Hiram, *Productivity Accounting*, Philadelphia : University of Pennsylvania Press, 1955.

Drtina, Ralph E., and Robert L. Porter, "Controlling R&D Spending," *Management Accounting* (May 1991), pp. 25-29.

Dunn, Robert M. Jr., and Salih N. Neftci, *Economic Growth Among Industrialized Countries : Why the United States Lags*, Washington, D.C. : National Planning Association, 1980.

Financial Accounting Standards Board, "Accounting for Research and Development Cost," *Statement of Financial Accounting Standards No. 2.* Stamford, Conn. : FASB, 1974.

_____. "Consolidation of All Majority-Owned Subsidiaries," *Statement of Financial Accounting Standards No. 94.* Stamford, Conn. : FASB, 1987.

_____. "Statement of Cash Flows," *Statement of Financial Accounting Standards No. 95.* Stamford, Conn. : FASB, 1987.

Freedman, Audrey, *Productivity Needs of the United States*, New York : The Conference Board, Inc., 1989.

Fusfeld, Daniel R, *Economic,* Lexington, Massachusetts : D.C. Heath and Company, 1972.

Gale, Bradley T. "Can More Capital Buy Higher Productivity?" *Harvard Business Review* (July-August 1980), pp. 78-86.

Ghemawat, Pankaj, and Richard E. Caves, "Capital Commitment and Profitability : An Empirical Investigation," *Oxford Economic Papers* (November 1986), pp. 94-110.

Gold, Bela, *Foundations of Productivity Analysis,* Pittsburgh : University of Pittsburgh Press, 1955.

_____. and Ralph M. Kraus, "Integrating Physical with Financial Measures for Managerial Controls," *Journal of Academy of Management* (June 1964), pp. 109-127.

_____. "Productivity Analysis and System Coherence," *Operational Research Quantity* (September 1965), pp. 287-307.

_____. *Productivity, Technology, and Capital.* Lexington, Massachusetts : D.C. Health and Company, 1979.

_____. "Practical Productivity Analysis for Management Accountants," *Management Accounting* (May 1980), pp.31-44.

Hendricks, James A., "Factory Automation," *Management Accounting* (December 1988), pp. 24-30.

Howell, Robert A., James D. Brown, Stephen R. Soucy, and Allen H. Seed, *Management Accounting in the New Manufacturing Environment,* New Jersey : National Association of Accountants, 1988.

_____. and Stephen Soucy, *Factory 2000+,* New Jersey : National Association of Accountants, 1988.

Kaplan, Robert S., "Measuring Manufacturing Performance : A New Challenge for Managerial Accounting Research," *The Accounting Review* (October 1983), pp. 686-705.

_____. "Variable and Self-Service Costs in Reciprocal Allocation Models," *The Accounting Review* (October 1973), pp. 739-748.

Keegan, Daniel P., Robert G. Eiler, and Joseph V. Anania, "The Factory of the Future," *Management Accounting* (December 1988), pp. 31-37.

Kendrick, John W., *Productivity Trends in the United States*, Princeton : Princeton University Press, for the National Bureau of Economic Research, 1961.

_____. *The National Wealth of the United States*, New York : The Conference Board, Inc., 1976.

_____. *An Introduction to the Dynamics of Productivity Change*, Baltimore, Maryland : The Johns Hopkins University Press, 1977.

_____. and Elliot S. Grossman, *Productivity in the United States Trends and Cycles*, Baltimore : The John Hopkins University Press, 1980.

_____. *Interindustry Differences in Productivity Growth*, Washington, D.C. : American Enterprise Institute, 1983.

_____. *Improving Company Productivity*, Baltimore: The Johns Hopkins University Press, 1984.

Lieberman, Marvin B. "Capacity Utilization : Theoretical Models and Empirical Tests," *European Journal of Operational Research* (1989), pp. 155-168.

Mammone, James L., "Productivity Measurement : A Conceptual Overview," *Management Accounting* (June 1980a), pp. 36-42.

_____. "Practical Approach to Productivity Measurement," *Management Accounting* (July 1980b), pp. 40-44.

Maysek, Peter, and Richard Fleming, "Tachometer Inspection," *Quality* (July 1980), pp. 40-44.

McClave, James T., and P. George Benson, *Statistics for Business and Economics*, San Francisco : Dellen Publishing Co., 1988.

McInnes, J. Morris, "Corporate Management of Productivity — An Empirical Study," *Strategic Management Journal* (March 1983), pp. 351-635.

Miller, David M., "Profitability = Productivity + Price Recovery," *Harvard Business Review* (May-June 1984), pp. 145-153.

_____. "Analyzing Total Factor Productivity With ROI as a Criterion," *Management Science* (November 1987), pp. 1501-1505.

_____. and Mohan P. Rao, "Analysis of Profit-Linked Total Factor Productivity Measurement Models : at the Firm Level," *Management Science* (June 1989), pp. 757-767.

Morbey, Graham K., and Robert M. Reithner, "How R&D Affects Sales Growth, Productivity, and Profitability," *Research-Technology Management* (May-June 1990), pp. 11-14.

Mundel, Marvin E., *Improving Productivity and Effectiveness*, Englewood Cliffs, NJ : Prentice-Hall, 1983.

Nadler, Leonard, "Human Resources Development and Productivity : Allied Forces," *Training & Development Journal* (August 1988), pp. 25-29.

Nelson, Randy A., "On the Measurement of capacity Utilization," *The Journal of Industrial Economics* (March 1989), pp. 273-286.

Rahman, Mawdudr, and A. R. Chowdhury, "Changes in R&D Expenditure and Productivity Growth : A Causal Analysis," *Arkansas Business & Economic Review* (1988), pp. 19-27.

Rzasa, Philip V., and Terrence W. Faulkner, "Analysis R&D Portfolios at Eastman Kodak," *Research-Technology Management* (January-February 1990), pp. 27-32.

Solow, Rebort M., "Technical Change and the Aggregate Production Function," *The Review of Economics and Statistics* (1957), pp. 312-320.

Sourwine, Darrel A., "Ensuring Financial As Well As Operational Success of Productivity Improvement Projects," *Industrial Engineering* (July 1988), pp. 34-40.

Terleckyj, Nestor E., "What do R&D Numbers Tell Us About Technological Change ?" *American Economic Association* (May 1980), pp. 55-61.

Thor, Carl G., "Employee Involvement and Productivity Gainsharing," *Industrial Management* (July-August 1987), pp. 21-25.

Ullmann, John E., *The Improvement of Productivity*, New York : Praeger Publishers, 1980.

U.S. Department of Commerce. *Bureau of Economic Analysis. Business Statistics (1961-1988)*, Washington, D.C.: U.S. Government Printing Office, December 1989.

Wait, Donald J., "Productivity Measurement : A Management Accounting Challenge," *Management Accounting* (May 1980), pp. 24-30.

Wilson, Marilyn, "Business Big Bet on New Equipment," *Dun's Business Month* (November 1984), pp. 40-45.

Index

For Product Safety Concerns and Information please contact our EU
representative GPSR@taylorandfrancis.com Taylor & Francis Verlag GmbH,
Kaufingerstraße 24, 80331 München, Germany

Printed and bound by CPI Group (UK) Ltd, Croydon, CR0 4YY
08/05/2025
01864450-0001